BEGINNERS GUIDE TO MICROPROCESSORS AND COMPUTING

by
E.F. SCOTT, M.Sc., C.Eng., M.I.E.R.E.

BERNARD BABANI (publishing) LTD
THE GRAMPIANS
SHEPHERDS BUSH ROAD
LONDON W6 7NF
ENGLAND

This book is based on a publication entitled *Introduction to Microprocessors and Computing,* which was produced as a limited edition by the author.

The author and publishers would like to thank the INTEL CORPORATION for allowing the reproduction of certain instruction set codes and descriptions given in the MCs 8080/85 manual, to be used in this book.

First Published – February 1980

Reprinted – March 1982

British Library Cataloguing in Publication Data

Scott, Edwin F

Beginners guide to microprocessors and computing.
(Bernards & Babani Press radio and electronics books; BP66).
1. Electronic digital computers
I. Title
001. 6'4044 QA76.5

ISBN 0 900162 87 2

Printed and Manufactured in Great Britain by Hunt Barnard Printing Ltd., Aylesbury, Bucks.

PREFACE

As indicated by the title, this book is intended as an introduction to the basic theory and concepts of binary arithmetic, microprocessor operation, and machine language programming. An attempt has been made to keep the style of presentation informal, but it is expected that the true newcomer to this field of study will need to follow the text carefully.

It is also expected that a reader with some knowledge of electronic theory may thirst for more detailed information concerning circuitry. This has been deliberately avoided in order that the text could be more pallatable and to take advantage of the "system approach" which modern integrated circuit* packages make possible. For those readers who wish to gain more detailed information about conventional electronic devices and circuits a selection of books is suggested at the rear of this book.

Although the technology used for integrated circuits has a great significance for the device performance, it is not essential to have knowledge of technology types to understand the operation. Many technologies exist now, and new ones are being developed continually by manufacturers so this area is confusing, even to the professional. For these reasons it is also wise to leave these aspects for more detailed study elsewhere.

There are occasions in the text where some background information might be helpful. A Glossary is given and an asterisk is used where it is thought helpful, to indicate words in the text which are included. It is in fact recommended to read the section on LOGIC as a warming up exercise. The glossary is also intended to be instructive and some terms included form an extention to the main text.

The only prior knowledge which has been assumed is very basic arithmetic, and an understanding of indices. The book should, therefore, prove useful for pupils preparing for C.S.E. and O-level examinations in addition to technicians, engineers and hobbyists. The "systems approach" and glossary of terms will be useful in the classroom to meet the trend in the 11-16 age group science curriculum.

This book aims to give an understanding of the basic principles of microprocessor operation, but it must be stated that detailed and intimate knowledge of the behaviour and performance of a particular device can only come from the manufacturer's literature and prolonged experience in using the device.

The questions given at the end of this book are designed to focus attention on the essential ideas developed in the text.

E. F. SCOTT

CONTENTS

CHAPTER 1

BINARY ARITHMETIC AND CODES

Because man has ten fingers it has proved convenient over the centuries to develop a number system based on ten. This is the well known decimal system, also known as denary. Our present number system is derived from the Hindus of Northern India dated back to at least 300 BC. There were other number systems prior to this, as for instance that used by the Chinese. However, the important feature of the Hindu system was a symbol to represent zero. The decimal system, as we all know, uses the position of a digit in a number to indicate whether it represents units, tens, hundreds and so on. Each position, or column, in fact represents increasing powers of 10 moving from right to left, i.e. 10^0, 10^1, 10^2, 10^3 etc. In other words a *base 10* system.

Binary arithmetic is a base 2 system in which the position of the digits represent powers of 2, i.e. 2^0, 2^1, 2^2, 2^3 etc. In the decimal system the largest digit which can exist in any column is the number nine, one less than the base. So with the binary system the largest digit which can occur in any position, before causing the 'carry one' to the next position, is one less than the base of 2, i.e. 1. In the decimal system the 'one' which is carried to the next column actually represents ten, or a hundred, etc. depending upon which column generates the carry. In the binary system the 'carry one' represents two, four, eight etc. depending upon the column generating the carry. In binary arithmetic there will only be two digits 0 and 1. It is this feature which makes the binary system so attractive for use in computers. Having just two positions, like ON and OFF, allows a series of switches to be used to indicate a number by having one position of each switch represent 1, and the other position '0'. This switch action leads to great accuracy because a definite action is required to operate a switch, it is highly unlikely to be operated in an accidental or spurious fashion. Having been operated the result is 100% accurate (a lamp, for example, is either OFF or ON, but not half on). Furthermore switches have great reliability and can operate correctly many thousands of times without failure. The 'switches' used in computers are electronic bistable* circuits, but the principle is identical to a light switch. So if we are to do 'sums' with computers we must understand binary arithmetic, particularly so if we hope to understand how they work.

The basic format needs no explanation and a simple statement will suffice. A subscript notation is used to indicate the base employed.

> 76_{10} means "seventy six" in decimal. Or . . . . "seven, six, in base ten"

> $1\ 0\ 1\ 0\ 1_2$ means "one, zero, one, zero, one, in binary" . . or base two.

2^4	2^3	2^2	2^1	2^0
1	0	1	0	1

$$= 2^0 + 2^2 + 2^4$$

$$= 1_{10} + 4_{10} + 16_{10} = \underline{\underline{21}}_{10}$$

Binary Addition

The technique is the same as for addition in decimal, except that two or more involves a carry process to the next column or columns. When dealing with binary addition it is wise to concentrate on the values of the columns, 1, 2, 4, 8, 16, etc., to avoid lapsing into decimal thinking.

Example

Decimal Addition

3	6	=	32 + 4
2	2	=	16 + 4 + 2
1	5	=	8 + 4 + 2 + 1
$_2$	7	=	4 + 2 + 1
8	0_{10}		

Binary Addition

	1	0	0	1	0	0
		1	0	1	1	0
			1	1	1	1
				1	1	1
1	1	11	1		1	
1	0	1	0	0	0	0_2

$$64_{10} + 16_{10} = 80_{10}$$

Notice that the 2 column and the 4 column give an overflow, or carry, of two columns. This is like adding a units column in decimal which totals over one hundred.

Binary Subtraction
This can be performed in exactly the same way as decimal.

Decimal	Binary	Binary	Decimal
2 $_{1}$3	1 0 1 1 1	1 1 $_{1}$0 1 1	2 7
−	−	−	−
1$_{1}$ 7	1 0 0 0 1	$_{1}$ 1 0 1	5
6	0 0 1 1 0	1 0 1 1 0	2 2

To gain practice in performing binary addition and subtraction the reader can create examples by converting decimal values to binary, and checking the results.

Before dealing with multiplication and division it must be understood that 'fractions' can be indicated by use of a point similar to the well known 'decimal point'. In this case, however, it is a 'binary point'. The positions following the point represent powers of 2 with a negative index.

$$1\,1\,0\,1\,.\,1\,1\,0\,1_2 = 2^3 + 2^2 + 2^0 + 2^{-1} + 2^{-2} + 2^{-4}\quad{}_{10}$$

$$= 8 + 4 + 1 + \tfrac{1}{2} + \tfrac{1}{4} + \tfrac{1}{16}\quad{}_{10}$$

When meeting binary fractions for the first time it is a little difficult to avoid thinking in terms of the more familiar decimal notation. It is perhaps helpful to remember when moving to the left from the binary point that the positions increase by a factor of x 2, whilst moving to the right the positions decrease by a factor ÷ 2. Thus moving the binary point one place to the right multiplies the binary number by 2, and moving the point to the left divides the binary number by 2. This of course is just like the decimal system where moving the point multiplies and divides by a factor of 10.

Actually the purist would argue that the numbers are moved past the decimal, or binary, point. But that is an arithmetic debate we will avoid. Most people understand the idea of moving the point.

Binary Multiplication
Because only ones and zeroes exist in binary the multiplication process is extremely simple compared with decimal multiplication. There are no 'tables' to remember!

Example

Decimal.

Multiplicant	3 . 7 5	4 'decimal places'
Multiplier	x 3 . 7 5	
Partial Products	1 8 7 5	
	2 6 2 5 0	add
	1 1 2 5 0 0	
	1 4 . 0 6 2 5	

4 decimal places

Binary

Multiplicant	1 1 . 1 1	4 'binary places'
Multiplier	x 1 1 . 1 1	
Partial Products	1 1 1 1	add
	1 1 1 1 0	
	1 1 1 1 0 0	
	$_1 1_{11} 1_1 1_1 1 0_1 0 0$	
	1 1 1 0 . 0 0 0 1	

4 binary places.

The binary process can be seen to consist only of shifting the multiplicant to the left and adding.

Binary Division

The technique here is the reverse of multiplication i.e. subtraction and shifting to the right.

Example.

Decimal 18.5 ÷ 2.

	1 0 0 1 . 0 1
	10_2) 1 0 0 1 0 . 1 0_2
Subtract divisor –	1 0
bring down next digit	0 0 0
Shift divisor →	1 0
Subtract divisor –	Does not, so put zero
bring down next digit	0 0 1
Shift divisor →	1 0
Subtract –	Does not, so put zero
bring down next digit	0 1 0
Shift divisor →	1 0
Subtract –	0 0
bring down next digit	0 0 1
Shift divisor →	1 0
Subtract –	Does not, so put zero
bring down next digit	0 1 0
Shift divisor →	1 0
Subtract –	0 0

These few examples suggest that the electronics involved will consist of *adder* circuits, and *shift* registers, which may sound vaguely familiar to some. Only the subtraction process seems to offer problems, and the need to identify and handle negative values. There is no need for panic however because there are a few more mathematical tricks which can be performed to electronic advantage.

One's Complement.

The 'one's complement' (1's C) of a binary number is obtained by subtracting each digit of the number from 1.

Thus:– 1's C of 1 = 1 – 1 = 0

1's C of 0 = 1 – 0 = 1

So to obtain the 1's C of a number (binary) it should be subtracted from all 1's. i.e.:–

```
1 1 1 1 1 1 1 1
1 0 0 1 1 0 0 1
---------------
0 1 1 0 0 1 1 0   1's C of 1 0 0 1 1 0 0 1
```

The 1's C is in fact seen to be simply the 'complement' of a number . . . . change all 0's to 1's, and 1's to 0's.

Now an interesting feature of 1's C can be demonstrated.

Consider $55_{10} - 25_{10} = 30_{10}$

```
1 1 0 1 1 1
0 1 1 0 0 1  –
-----------
0 1 1 1 1 0₂
```

Now taking the complement of 0 1 1 0 0 1 and *adding* to 1 1 0 1 1 1, and then performing what is known as an "end around carry" (E.A.C.) (Notice the smaller number is subtracted from the larger number. It is therefore the smaller number which is converted to 1's C. This always results in an *overflow* when the addition is performed).

```
                 1 1 0 1 1 1
                               +
Complement       1 0 0 1 1 0

Overflow       [1] 0 1 1 1 0 1
                               +
E.A.C.          └──────────► 1
               ---------------
                 0 1 1 1 1 0
```

So using 1's complement it is possible to perform subtraction by use of an addition process. This is good news for computer electronics.

Negative Numbers

Everything so far has been quite straightforward because only positive numbers have been considered. There will however be occasions when a computer calculation will involve negative quantities. Some arrangement must therefore be made to distinguish positive values from negative values. The most elementary way to do this is by reserving the most significant bit in a binary number as a sign indicator, a 1 for negative and an 0 for positive. The most significant bit is the '1' or '0' at the extreme left of the binary number. It is commonly referred to as M.S.B. The least significant bit (L.S.B.) is to the extreme right.

$$+20_{10} = 0\ 0\ 0\ 1\ 0\ 1\ 0\ 0_2$$

$$-20_{10} = 1\ 0\ 0\ 1\ 0\ 1\ 0\ 0_2$$

This method of indicating the sign of a number is called 'SIGN MAGNITUDE'. The first bit indicates sign and the remainder give the magnitude in binary.

In a computer the binary numbers are contained and manipulated in *registers**. A register consists of a number of bistable* elements to represent the 1's and 0's. For the organisation of the computer operation it is clear that the registers must have some fixed length. This varies from 32 bits* on large mainframe machines down to typically 8 (or even four) on small micro-computers.

The maximum number (N) of 1's and 0's combinations which can be contained by a register of n bits is given by :–

$$N = 2^n$$

For example consider a simple 3-bit register. The possible alternatives are :–

000, 001, 010, 011, 100, 101, 110, 111.

$N = 2^3$ or 8_{10}

N of course will include zero. Therefore the greatest number (M) which can be contained in a register will be given by:–

$$M = (2^n - 1)$$

In the case of the 3-bit register the maximum number which can be represented will be 7_{10}, or $1\ 1\ 1_2$.

Using 'sign magnitude' will result in the loss of one bit so far as the magnitude of the number is concerned. Using sign magnitude therefore the greatest value which can be held by a register will be given by:–

$$\pm M = \pm(2^{n-1} - 1)$$

where n = the total number of bits in the register, one of which is now allocated to indicate the sign.

A computer could be organised to express positive numbers in sign magnitude and negative numbers in 1's C, the most significant bit (M.S.B.) again being used to indicate the sign. This would allow the 1's C of subtraction already discussed to be used. Unfortunately there are two undesirable features.

i) there will be two ways of expressing zero, viz:–

0 0 0 0 0 0 0 0 and 1 1 1 1 1 1 1 1

+0, and –0 respectively.

ii) Subtraction using 1's C for two numbers A and B is not valid when A = B. This is demonstrated below.

correct	correct	incorrect
$7_{10} = 1\ 1\ 1$	$7 = 1\ 1\ 1$	$7 = 1\ 1\ 1$
$4_{10} = 1\ 0\ 0$ (−)	1's C of 4 0 1 1 (+)	1'sC of 7 0 0 0 (+)
$1\ 1 = 3_{10}$	[1] 0 1 0	[ ] 1 1 1
	E.A.C. → 1 (+)	E.A.C. is not generated.
	1 1	

A solution to these problems is to express negative numbers in 2's C. The 2's C of a number is obtained by adding 1 to the 1's C. Thus:–

2's C of 15_{10} = (1'sC of 1 1 1 1) + 1

```
=     0 0 0 0
              +
      0 0 0 1
      -------
      0 0 0 1
      =======
```

Using 2's C arithmetic the positive numbers are the same as for 'sign magnitude' and the 2's C is taken for negative numbers.

```
+72₁₀    = 0¦1 0 0 1 0 0 0

−95₁₀    = 1¦0 1 0 0 0 0 1....

ie 1's C = 0 1 0 0 0 0 0
                        +
                       1
           -------------
           0 1 0 0 0 0 1 = 2's C of 95₁₀
```

Adding 72_{10} and -95_{10}

```
0¦1 0 0 1 0 0 0
               +
1¦0 1 0 0 0 0 1
---------------
1¦1 1 0 1 0 0 1  Answer in 2's C.
```

Converting this answer to 1's C, by subtracting 1, and then taking the complement will give the binary form which can then be converted to the familiar decimal form in which we can verify the 2's C answer. The sign bit is not significant so far as the magnitude of the answer is concerned.

	1 ¦ 1 1 0 1 0 0 1
Subtract 1	1
	1 ¦ 1 1 0 1 0 0 0
Complement	¦ 0 0 1 0 1 1 1
	↓ ↓ ↓ ↓
Decimal values	16 4 2 1 = -23_{10}

So adding positive numbers would involve straight forward addition of sign magnitude, i.e. binary numbers. When adding a negative quantity it would be necessary to take the 2's C of the negative number and add. To subtract, the 2's C value of the number to be subtracted (subtrahend) would be added to the other number (minuend) given in sign magnitude. It is important to notice that when performing any of these routines both numbers are considered as having a particular, and identical bit length.

Examples: Check by converting to decimal.

Addition

Two positive numbers	0 ¦ 1 0 1 0 1	+
	0 ¦ 1 0 0 0 1	
$21_{10} + 17_{10}$	1 ¦ 0 0 1 1 0	The carry into the sign bit represents an 'overflow'.

Positive and negative number	0 ¦ 1 0 1 0 1 +
	1 ¦ 0 1 1 1 1
$21_{10} + (-17_{10})$	1 ← 0 ¦ 0 0 1 0 0 = $+4_{10}$

The carry generated through the sign bit is ignored because the positive number is greater than the negative number. The answer is given directly in binary

$17_{10} + (-21_{10})$

$$\begin{array}{r} 0\,|\,1\,0\,0\,0\,1 \\ 1\,|\,0\,1\,0\,1\,1 \\ \hline 1\,|\,1\,1\,1\,0\,0 \end{array} + \quad \text{2's C result}$$

No carry bit is generated through the sign bit in this case and the sign bit is correct. The magnitude, however, is in 2's C. A method of obtaining the binary value from a 2's C value is to simply add 1 to the least significant bit of the complemented value.

Thus in this case

$$1\,|\,1\,1\,1\,0\,0 \qquad \begin{array}{r} 1\,|\,0\,0\,0\,1\,1 \\ 1 \\ \hline 1\,|\,0\,0\,1\,0\,0 \end{array} + \; = -4_{10}$$

All that has been done so far is to show how a computer (micro*, or otherwise) can manipulate binary numbers to perform calculations. Computers are generally thought of as machines for doing calculations, simple or complicated. Many computers are indeed employed solely for this purpose. Adding up and subtracting deposits and withdrawals at the bank for customer's accounts and providing a *print-out*, . . . the dreaded bank statement is an obvious example. However, many computers, particularly minis* and micros, are employed to control processes, or monitor physical conditions or events. In other words run and organise engineering systems of one sort or another. This is not to say that calculations could not be involved. A study of the tricks of binary arithmetic will therefore be useful in this connection. But binary arithmetic serves another useful purpose in that it introduces quite clearly the fundamental idea of two-state devices (electronic bistable circuits) being used as memory *cells* which can contain a 'bit' of information, i.e. a 1 or a 0. Also the idea of using a number of these cells to contain a complete binary number, or character, which can then be manipulated. Perhaps the bits contained are to be shifted to the left, or right, or added bit by bit to another character, or number. The group of cells used to contain characters, and which can be manipulated in some way is called a *register*. Most micro-computers (microprocessors) employ 8 bit registers, 12 bit, or 16 bit machines are, however, available. Obviously larger numbers can be manipulated in the latter cases (remember the 2^n, or 2^{n-1} relationship?), but as we shall see the greater number of bits can have other advantages. The bistable elements, or cells, may not be physically arranged in rows but for the sake of our sanity we will have a mental picture of a register as shown in figure 1.1. This register is seen to have an additional bit into which the register can overflow. This is not essential for all registers, but it will sometimes be useful. This is particularly useful for registers which are to receive the result of a calculation.

Fig. 1.1 *An 8-bit register with an additional bit to contain an "overflow".*

CODES

As one might imagine, mere humans will find all these 'ones' and 'zeroes' rather clumsy to deal with mentally, or remember. Particularly in the case of 16, 24 or even 32 bit numbers. Of course when actually doing calculations with binary arithmetic there is no help for it, we will just have to slog away with long strings of 1's and 0's, and by the way we need to understand that this is also true for a computer. It is the 1's and 0's which a computer understands.

But it is possible to simplify the situation when referring to individual binary numbers, or patterns of 1's and 0's by use of a *coding system*. There are many ways of coding binary data but just a few which have found favour with manufacturers and in common use.

Octal

This coding system expresses the numerical value of a binary number, (or the equivalent numerical value of any pattern of 1's and 0's) in base eight. This we shall see proves to be very convenient for conversion to, or from, binary form. Something is already known about number systems having a particular base. We know that the position of the digits are arranged in ascending powers of the base number. In this case, 8^0, 8^1, 8^2, 8^3 and so on. It is also understood that the maximum number which will occur will be one less than the base number, in this case 7.

Taking a couple of simple examples to get us started.

$$0\ 2\ 0_8 = 16_{10}$$

$$0\ 2\ 3_8 = 19_{10}$$

$$4\ 2\ 6_8 = 4 \times 8^2 + 2 \times 8^1 + 6 \times 8^0 = 278_{10}$$

An 'octal point' can also be employed like a decimal point and a binary point, to express fractions in the order 8^{-1}, 8^{-2}, 8^{-3}, etc., i.e. $\frac{1}{8}$, $\frac{1}{64}$, . . .

0.4 in octal means $4 \times \frac{1}{8}$, or 4×8^{-1}

$36.21_8 = 24 + 6 + \frac{1}{4} + \frac{1}{16}$ in decimal.

It will now be interesting to see how much time, space and ink we save by using octal coding.

Not a lot of difference between octal and decimal it would seem. There are three digits in each case. But there is a saving compared with binary.

$$278_{10} = 426_8 = 1\ 0\ 0\ 0\ 1\ 0\ 1\ 1\ 0_2$$

There is, however, a great advantage in the use of octal rather than decimal because it is very easy to do the conversion from octal to binary, and binary to octal. Examination of the example above shows that there are 3 binary digits for each octal digit. By knowing the binary equivalents of digits 0 – 7 therefore it is an easy job to do the conversion. The process is illustrated actually on page 14.

Octal value	7	3	0	4	5
Binary value	(1 1 1)	(0 1 1)	(0 0 0)	(1 0 0)	(1 0 1)$_2$

likewise $1\,0\,1\,0\,1\,1\,1\,1\,1\,0\,1\,0\,0\,1\,0\,1\,1_2$
and grouping in threes
$2\quad 5\quad 7\quad 5\quad 1\quad 3_8$

Decimal to octal and octal to decimal is not quite so easy.

Decimal to octal conversion :— divide by eight (÷ 8) continually, and write out the remainders. As usual an example will explain it best.

```
8 ) 198         ↑ L.S.B.
8 )  24 r 6     |
8 )   3 r 0     |
      0 r 3     | M.S.B.
```

$\therefore 198_{10} = 306_8$

To convert a decimal fraction to an octal fraction the inverse of this operation is used. The fraction is continually multiplied by eight and a note made of the 'spillover', or overflow.

To convert $.365_{10}$ to octal.

```
              3 6 5
M.S.B.          x 8
|        2 ← 9 2 0
|               x 8
|        7 ← 3 6 0
|               x 8
|        2 ← 8 8 0
|               x 8
|        7 ← 0 4 0
|               x 8
↓        0 ← 3 2 0
L.S.B.             etc.
```

$.365_{10} = .27270\ldots\ldots_8$

When converting from decimal to octal it is necessary to deal with the integers (whole numbers) and fractions (decimal places) separately.

Hexadecimal

This code uses a base of 16. A little thought here will indicate a problem of notation. Using the digits available in the familiar decimal system will give double figures from 10 to 15. To overcome this we borrow a few symbols from another familiar source, the alphabet. Ten (10) becomes A, eleven (11) becomes B, twelve (12) becomes C . . . etc. The symbols 0 – 15 for hexadecimal, or 'hex' code are shown below, along with their binary equivalent.

Decimal		Hex.		Binary
0	=	0	=	0 0 0 0
1	=	1	=	0 0 0 1
2	=	2	=	0 0 1 0
3	=	3	=	0 0 1 1
4	=	4	=	0 1 0 0
5	=	5	=	0 1 0 1
6	=	6	=	0 1 1 0
7	=	7	=	0 1 1 1
8	=	8	=	1 0 0 0
9	=	9	=	1 0 0 1
10	=	A	=	1 0 1 0
11	=	B	=	1 0 1 1
12	=	C	=	1 1 0 0
13	=	D	=	1 1 0 1
14	=	E	=	1 1 1 0
15	=	F	=	1 1 1 1
16	=	10	=	1 0 0 0 0
17	=	11	=	1 0 0 0 1
:				
36	=	24	=	1 0 0 1 0 0
				etc.

Table 1.1 The hexadecimal code

The hexadecimal table indicates a further simplification of binary numbers. Each hexadecimal digit represents four binary digits. Conversion from binary to hex, or hex to binary, therefore involves groupings of 4 binary digits instead of 3, as for octal.

Example. **HEX TO BINARY**

HEX	7	A	B	3
BINARY	0 1 1 1	1 0 1 0	1 0 1 1	0 0 1 1

BINARY TO HEX

1	0 1 1 1	1 1 0 1	1 0 0 1	1 1 0 1
1	1	D	9	D

The letter H is usually used to indicate a hexadecimal value. The hexadecimal value in the above example would be written:

$11D9D_H$

To convert a decimal number to Hex, requires a similar operation to that used for converting decimal to octal, except that division by sixteen is used.

Converting 356_{10} to HEX

16	) 3 5 6	
16	) 2 2	4 remainder
16	) 1	6 remainder
	0	1 remainder

$356_{10} = 164_H$

Conversion of a decimal fraction to a hex. fraction requires multiplication by sixteen and noting the overflow.

Thus to convert $.125_{10}$ to hex.

```
 .1 2 5
  x 1 6
 ------
  7 5 0
1 2 5 0
 ------
2.0 0 0
```

i.e. $.125_{10} = .2_H$

Converting $.34_{10}$ to hex

```
   . 3 4
   x 1 6
 -------
 5 . 4 4
   x 1 6
 -------
 7 . 0 4
   x 1 6
 -------
       etc.
```

i.e. $.34_{10} = .57_H$

This is seen to be rather clumsy with 16 being a double figure. It is for this reason that conversion tables are found useful.

Conversion of both hex., and octal, to decimal can be accomplished by first making the simple conversion to binary (groups of 4 or 3 respectively) and then converting the binary to decimal.

Binary to Decimal Conversion

For converting integers a method is based on the fact that 5 binary places represents 32_{10}. It is, therefore, merely necessary to split the binary value into groups of five and multiply each decimal equivalent of each group by 32 raised to the appropriate power. Finally, the separate decimal values are added.

Thus $\overbrace{101}^{32^2}\ \overbrace{01110}^{32^1}\ \overbrace{11001}^{32^0}$

$$5 \times 32^2 + 14 \times 32^1 + 21 \times 32^0 =$$

$$5 \times 1024 + 14 \times 32 + 21 \times 1 = 5589_{10}$$

Conversion of binary fractions to decimal fractions is best performed by summing the decimal equivalent value for each binary position.

Thus

$$
\begin{aligned}
& .\ 1\ 1\ 0\ 1\ 1\ 0\ 1_2 \\
&= \tfrac{1}{2} + \tfrac{1}{4} + \tfrac{1}{16} + \tfrac{1}{32} + \tfrac{1}{128} \\
&= 0.5 + .25 + .0625 + .03125 + .0078125 = 0.8515625_{10}
\end{aligned}
$$

Some microprocessor and computer manufacturers have adopted octal coding to express binary quantities, and bit patterns, others have chosen hex. coding. In either case it serves to simplify the identification and writing of binary, the 'machine code' is still binary. (See MACHINE. LANGUAGE*).

Binary Coded Decimal (B.C.D.)

A series of 4 bistable circuits (electronic 'switches' having two possible states) would normally have a total of 0 – 15 equivalent decimal values. By arranging the 4 elements in 'series' or 'cascade'* a *counter* can be formed to count electrical signals, or pulses applied to the first bistable element. The sixteenth pulse would return all 4 elements to the 0 state and a pulse would be passed to the next series of elements forming a second counter. In other words, pulses could be counted in hexadecimal. Light emitting diodes (LEDS*) could be used to indicate when a bistable element is in a 1 state.

Thus the L.E.D.s would indicate the number of pulses which had been applied i.e. counted. The series of diagrams (Fig. 1.2) shown on page 19 illustrate the principle.

Taking the illuminated L.E.D.s as 1's the L.E.D.s can be seen to be following the binary codes shown on page 15 for the hexadecimal notation. It is left to the reader to complete the missing diagrams for 5 to 15.

It is also found useful to express decimal numbers using only binary values of 1 and 0. To do this a four-bit code is arranged with each bit having a particular decimal value. Several different codings are possible:–

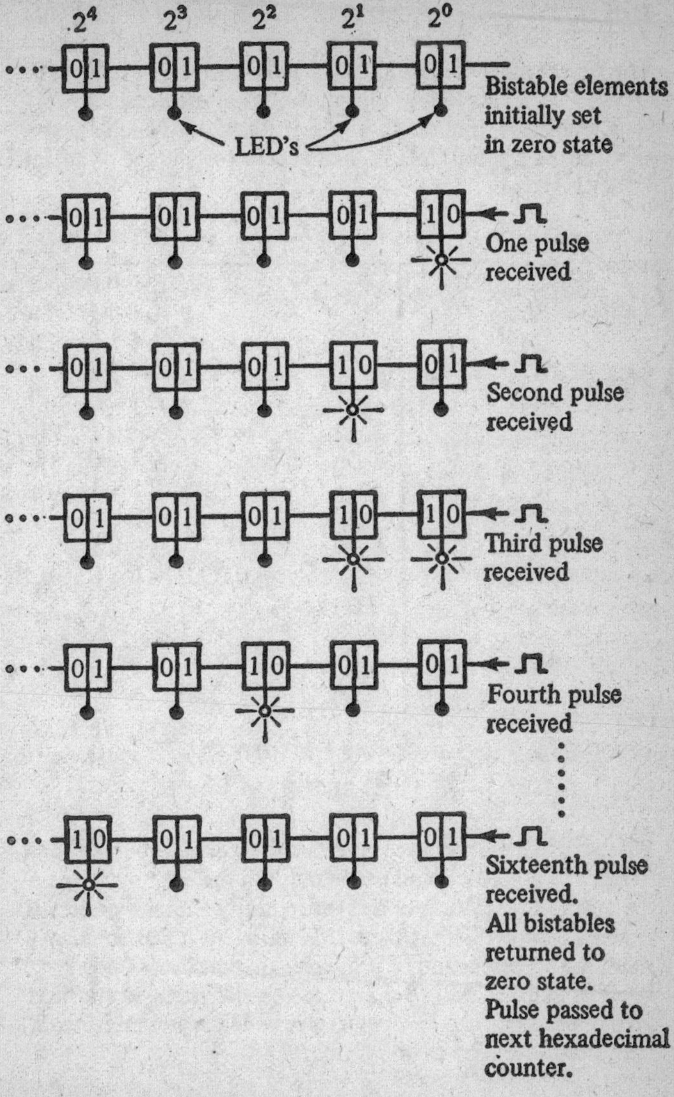

Fig. 1.2 *Bistable elements used to form a hexadecimal counter.*

8 4 2 1   5 2 1 1   2 4 2 1

The first is most commonly used and examples of its use are shown below. Further groups of 4 bits are used to indicate tens, hundreds, thousands, etc. A truth table* which shows the state of the four bits in each decade for a range of decimal values is shown.

DECIMAL VALUE	8 4 2 1 B. C. D.			
0			0 0 0 0	←pulses
1			0 0 0 1	1st
2			0 0 1 0	2nd
3			0 0 1 1	
4			0 1 0 0	
5			0 1 0 1	
6			0 1 1 0	
7			0 1 1 1	
8			1 0 0 0	
9			1 0 0 1	
10		0 0 0 1	0 0 0 0	· 10th
•				
•				
48		0 1 0 0	1 0 0 0	
•				
•				
736	0 1 1 1	0 0 1 1	0 1 1 0	

Table 1.2

The hexadecimal counters considered earlier can be modified to reset to all zeroes, and pass a pulse to the next counter on the tenth pulse. This is done electronically and circuit details are best dealt with elsewhere. It is sufficient for us to understand in this discussion of principles that a Binary Coded Decimal counter using 8 4 2 1 code can be arranged and that further counters can be used to give coded representation of tens, hundreds, and so on.

ASCII Code
The name of this code is derived from the initial letters of

"American Standard Code for Information Interchange." This is a coding system used to represent numerals, letters of the alphabet and a wide range of commonly used symbols such as plus and minus signs, commas, brackets, etc. This is not the only code in use for this purpose but it has become almost universally adopted. The need to have such a code will become clear in later discussion of computer systems. At this stage, however, it is sufficient to say that computer programming can be performed by entering statements such as A D D R_1 R_2, which the computer will understand to mean 'add the contents of register number one to the contents of register number two'. The letters, numbers, commas etc., are entered by an electronic keyboard which generates a series of pulses (1's and 0's) according to the ASCII code (table 1.3). Letters and numbers need to be typed by a printer* at the direction of a computer when it compiles a bank statement. So it is easy to see at this early stage the need to have a coding system for all the characters likely to be used. It would also be very convenient if manufacturers and users adopted the same code. Any manufacturer's printer could then be connected easily to any computer for example.

The electrical signals used to represent characters again employ the inherent accuracy and reliability we have come to associate with two-state systems. In this case the two states are voltage levels, 5 volts for a 1 state and 0 volts for a 0 state. The ASCII code shown by Table 1.3 is seen to be a seven bit code. The illustration below (Fig. 1.3) shows the series of electrical voltage levels which would be generated for the letter F, i.e. 1 0 0 0 1 1 0.

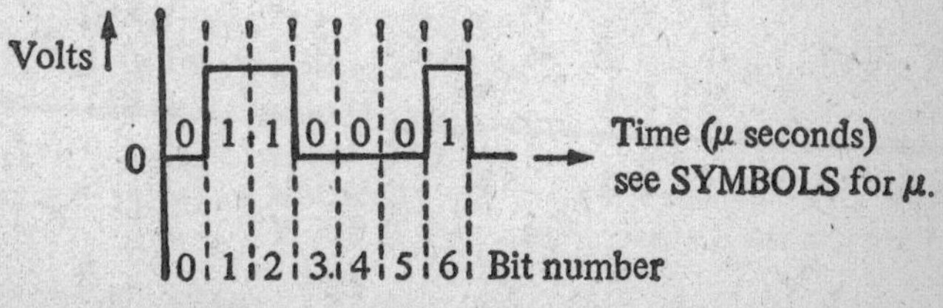

Fig. 1.3 Serial transmission of the letter 'F' in A.S.C.I.I. code.

The bits in a binary code, character or register, are usually identified by a number. In this seven bit case, 0 through 6.

0 1 0	0 0 1 1	#
0 1 0	0 1 0 0	$
0 1 0	0 1 0 1	%
0 1 0	0 1 1 0	&
0 1 0	0 1 1 1	'
0 1 0	1 0 0 0	(
0 1 0	1 0 0 1	)
0 1 0	1 0 1 0	*
0 1 0	1 0 1 1	+
0 1 0	1 1 0 0	,
0 1 0	1 1 0 1	-
0 1 0	1 1 1 0	.
0 1 0	1 1 1 1	/

0 1 1	0 0 0 0	0
0 1 1	0 0 0 1	1
0 1 1	0 0 1 0	2
0 1 1	0 0 1 1	3
0 1 1	0 1 0 0	4
0 1 1	0 1 0 1	5
0 1 1	0 1 1 0	6
0 1 1	0 1 1 1	7
0 1 1	1 0 0 0	8
0 1 1	1 0 0 1	9
0 1 1	1 0 1 0	:
0 1 1	1 0 1 1	;
0 1 1	1 1 0 0	<
0 1 1	1 1 0 1	=
0 1 1	1 1 1 0	>
0 1 1	1 1 1 1	?

1 0 0	0 0 0 0	@
1 0 0	0 0 0 1	A
1 0 0	0 0 1 0	B
1 0 0	0 0 1 1	C
1 0 0	0 1 0 0	D
1 0 0	0 1 0 1	E
1 0 0	0 1 1 0	F
1 0 0	0 1 1 1	G
1 0 0	1 0 0 0	H
1 0 0	1 0 0 1	I
1 0 0	1 0 1 0	J
1 0 0	1 0 1 1	K
1 0 0	1 1 0 0	L
1 0 0	1 1 0 1	M
1 0 0	1 1 1 0	N
1 0 0	1 1 1 1	O

1 0 1	0 0 0 0	P
1 0 1	0 0 0 1	Q
1 0 1	0 0 1 0	R
1 0 1	0 0 1 1	S
1 0 1	0 1 0 0	T
1 0 1	0 1 0 1	U
1 0 1	0 1 1 0	V
1 0 1	0 1 1 1	W
1 0 1	1 0 0 0	X
1 0 1	1 0 0 1	Y
1 0 1	1 0 1 0	Z
1 0 1	1 0 1 1	[
1 0 1	1 1 0 0	\
1 0 1	1 1 0 1	]
1 0 1	1 1 1 0	↑
1 0 1	1 1 1 1	←

Table 1.3 ASCII Codes for Numerals, Letters, and some Common Symbols.

Examination of the numbers 0 – 9 of the ASCII code shows the four least significant bits following the B.C.D. notation shown in Table 1.2. The letters A – Z also follow the same coding but with a change in the three most significant bits.

Additional bits can be added to an ASCII coded character to indicate the start of the character and its ending ('start' and 'stop' bits). Because it is possible for errors to occur in the transmission of electrical signals a further bit can be added to give an indication if an error has occurred. This bit is known as a 'parity bit'. The idea is to add a bit, if necessary, so that the total number of bits transmitted is either an odd number, or an even number. The two alternative methods are known as 'odd parity', or 'even parity' respectively. Extra circuitry is of course required to add the parity bit where necessary at the sending end, and to check the parity at the receiving end. All such sophisticated techniques mean more hardware and, therefore, more money. Certain integrated circuits* are available which are capable of adding parity to a character, or checking parity. One such device is the U.A.R.T. discussed in chapter 3.

Data Formats

The binary bits which make up a character, or binary number, can be transmitted in and out of the computer, or manipulated within the computer, in two ways, either serial or parallel. Serial data is moved bit by bit, perhaps it could be called 'in single file'. The bits will be moved at regular intervals under the control of an electronic timing clock circuit.

Parallel data refers to the movement of data character by character. In this case all the bits which make up a character are moved at the same instant. Obviously there will be a time advantage with the use of parallel data.

Fig. 1.4 illustrates the idea of serial and parallel transfer of binary data from a register.

Armed with these few basic ideas and a sneaky belief that electronics can do almost anything, we can plunge fearlessly into microprocessors and computing.

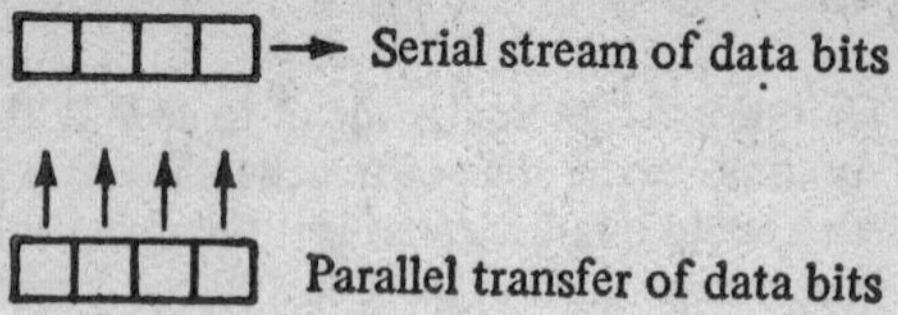

Fig. 1.4 Serial and parallel transfer of data.

CHAPTER 2

BASIC MICROPROCESSOR AND COMPUTER ARCHITECTURE

To understand the microprocessor it is really necessary to have at least a rudimentary idea of how a computer system is put together. This is because the microprocessor (μP) which is usually a 40 pin integrated circuit*(IC) only has any real value when it is used as a component part of a computing system. With technology advancing so rapidly however we have to be careful about such statements because as more and more functions have been incorporated into a single 'chip' (sometimes called a 'bug') the complete 'computer on a chip' has been approached. Regardless of this merging of functions we will again for sanity sake picture a computer system as shown in Fig. 2.1 consisting of four sections.

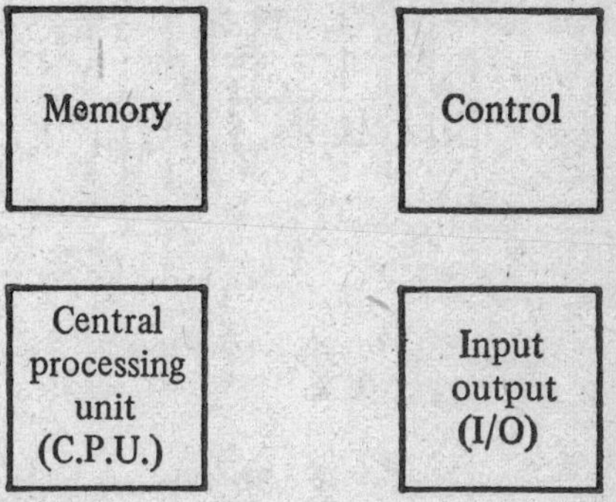

Fig. 2.1 The four sections of a computer.

Let's deal with each section in turn in just sufficient detail to get us along the road.

Memory
This is essentially a bank of binary cells which are arranged in groups just like a register. There are in fact hardware*

differences between memory cells and registers but the idea is the same. Each bistable cell can be set to store, or 'remember' a '1' or '0'. Thus a group of 8 memory cells can store a single 8 bit binary number, or pattern of 1's and 0's. It was pointed out earlier in chapter 1 that bits would not always represent a 'number' so from now on we will call the 8 bits collectively a 'character'*. 8 bits of binary data is also referred to as a 'byte'*.

The mental picture we need for a memory is shown in Fig.2.2. Each group of 8 cells forms a *location* in memory, and so that we know where each of the characters is stored in the memory each location is given an *address*. To do this the locations are simply numbered, starting at 0, as shown by the addresses marked to the right of each location in Fig. 2.2. Addresses too are usually referred to by their hexadecimal or octal value depending upon the code adopted by the manufacturer.

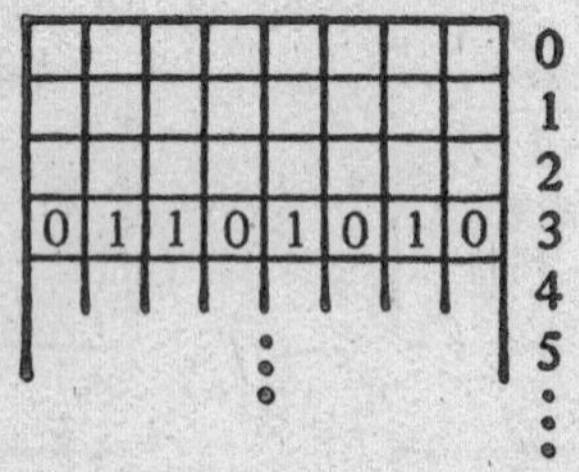

Fig. 2.2 *A section of memory showing 6 A_H stored in location No. 3.*

The various forms of memory which are available are discussed under MEMORY which appears in the glossary given at the rear. Do not confuse yourself with that just yet, it all looks like Fig. 2.2. To keep the record straight it might be wise to just admit at this point that a microprocessor chip could itself contain a limited amount of memory. How else could there be a "computer on a chip?"

Control

It is not necessary to have a degree in electronics to understand that some control must be exercised over a system which will be required to perform many different functions, at great speed, and in any one of a variety of sequences. There is little point in starting to add the contents of two registers together until the binary numbers have actually been entered into the registers. The control section must therefore supervise the timing of events. It will also be necessary to organise the movement of binary numbers in different ways depending on the function to be performed. For instance, adding two numbers in binary requires a different sequence of events to subtraction using 2's C.

To be strictly truthful all the electronics involved in these sort of control functions does not reside in one clearly defined unit, or section, as suggested by the block diagram. On the contrary, it is distributed throughout the computer. But our diagram is a sensible approach because it is our aim to clarify, not mistify.

Input/Output (I/O)

Although electronics and computing has generated an enormous amount of terminology, (some people might call it 'jargon'), much of it does at least have an obvious meaning. This is a good example of such a self-explanatory term. I/O is all that electronics which deals with getting information into the computer, and out of the computer. The Input/Output section forms an *interface** between the computer and the engine it is testing, the machinery it controls, or simply the electronic keyboard which has already been mentioned.

The I/O facilities are often provided by special families of electronic devices produced by the microprocessor manufacturer. One of the most common devices supplied by manufacturers is a Universal Asynchronous Receiver Transmitter (U.A.R.T.). This integrated circuit* converts serial data to parallel data, or parallel data to serial data. It also adds start, stop, and odd or even parity bits to a character.

As technologies improve more and more I/O facilities are being incorporated into the microprocessor chip. Examples of on-chip interface circuits now include serial or parallel binary input and output, and synchronising (clock) signals. However, despite this "board shrinking" process it is most usual to find the interfacing electronics outside the microprocessor chip, but included on the same board. Thus single board computers (S.B.C.) are very commonplace and might include the interfaces for connection to peripherals* such as teletypewriters*, cassette tape recorder, Video Display Unit (V.D.U.)*.

The Central Processing Unit (C.P.U.)
This section of a computer can be thought of as its heart. It is here that computation takes place. In short it is in the C.P.U. where the 'sums' are done. The C.P.U. does not, however, like a heart, work continuously and independently for it must work in association with the other three sections.

A microprocessor is capable of performing computation when combined with other devices and circuitry covering Memory, I/O, and Control. Many functions which might rightly be regarded as control are carried out by the microprocessor. It is for this reason that the control section in our understanding is going to be allowed to spill over into the C.P.U. (In any case we did say that control was distributed through the system). Including all the functions available in a microprocessor in the C.P.U. also ties in with the view of a microcomputer system held by many device manufacturers who refer to their microprocessor as a C.P.U.

A single microprocessor containing all the necessary control and some memory could be called a computer on a chip. Now that we have some idea of the role of each of these sections it is possible to consider the entire system in greater detail.

Two registers are associated with the memory, they are the Memory Address Register and the Memory Data Register. The M.A.R. and M.D.R. respectively. The M.A.R. is fed with the address of the location from which a character is to be taken, or in which a character is to be stored. Putting data into a register, or memory location, is usually called *loading*. The M.D.R. is loaded with the contents of the addressed memory location, or loaded with the binary character which is to be placed in the location addressed. The binary data bits are moved in parallel form with a conductor path for each bit. These paths are collectively known as a *bus**. Thus there will be two buses employed, one for the data and another for the address. The C.P.U. will load the M.A.R. with the appropriate address. The data will be passed back to the C.P.U. for processing from the M.D.R., or alternatively the C.P.U. will load the M.D.R. with the data to be loaded into the specified memory location. Figure 2.3 illustrates the flow of addresses and data in or out of the memory via the address and data bus.

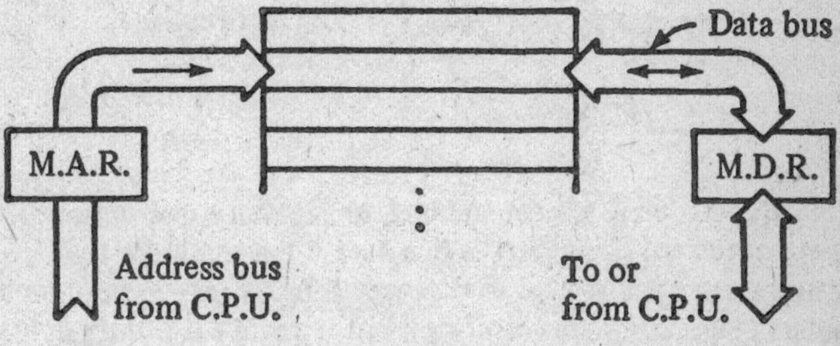

Fig. 2.3 *Address and data bus.*

Some locations in the memory will undoubtedly be used for storing numbers, but the memory must also contain the 'program' which the computer will execute. (At long last we meet that familiar word!). The memory can be described as an instruction sheet like those in a model aeroplane kit. The operations to be performed are set out in the correct sequence and numbered. The instructions are our program for making the model and we slavishly move through step by step from the beginning to the end. The locations in a computer memory contain the sequence of instructions which make a program. An instruction might be ADD, in which case this will be represented by a particular bit pattern, such as 1 0 0 0 0 0 0 1. The computer will understand this machine language* instruction. Clearly some way of stepping through the memory is required to bring out each instruction in turn via the M.D.R. for execution by the C.P.U.

The Program Counter is a register which initially contains the starting address of the program. This might be expected to be location zero, but the program could start elsewhere in memory. The program counter (P.C.) supplies the M.A.R. Each time an instruction is transferred to the M.D.R. the P.C. contents is advanced by one, the P.C. is said to be "incremented by one." In other words the P.C. acts as a counter. In this way the P.C. acts as a 'pointer' to the next instruction to be performed. This can be likened to our finger moving down the model kit instruction sheet.

Open box.
Lift out fuselage.
Lift out wing.
Fix wing A in slot B.
⋮

"Open box" may appear to be an unnecessary instruction. For the purpose of this example however it is a reminder that computers must be told to do everything. It may appear sometimes that a computer can think but in reality it is only doing what a programmer previously told it to do.

Although the instructions might conveniently and economically be restricted to 8 bits this would only allow a maximum of 256 locations to be addressed if the P.C. and M.A.R. were also 8 bit. To allow for more memory, and hence longer programs, the P.C., M.A.R., and therefore address bus of a microprocessor is 16 bit usually.

The situation now is illustrated by Fig. 2.4.

The instructions which make up the program are each represented by various bit-patterns. After fetching each instruction it is therefore necessary to *decode* this pattern of 1's and 0's. The decoding is performed by electronic logic* circuitry. To enter the instruction into the decode circuit a further register is employed, the Instruction Register (see Fig. 2.5).

A pair of numbers is usually associated with each instruction

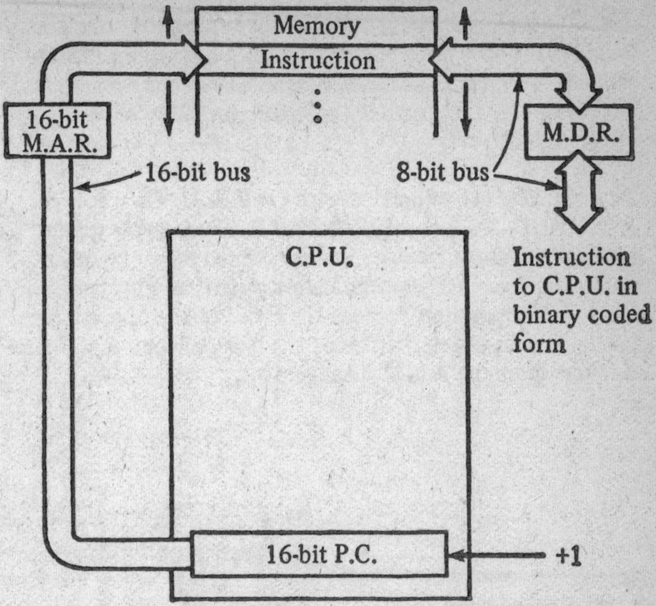

Fig. 2.4 *The use of the P.C. to "point" to the next instruction.*

such as ADD. To understand where the two numbers for adding will come from requires an understanding of another important section of the C.P.U., the *Arithmetic and Logic Unit.*

The Arithmetic and Logic Unit (A.L.U.)

This section of the C.P.U. consists of scores of electronic gates* and circuits which can be electronically arranged to perform one of many possible functions. One of these functions we might guess will be addition. When the ADD instruction appears in the Instruction Register (I.R.) the decode circuit provides the necessary signals to configure the A.L.U. as an ADDER circuit. If, however, the instruction was COMPARE then the decode circuit would configure the A.L.U. as a COMPARATOR. The various instructions which can be carried out by the A.L.U. will require the computer system to follow different sequences of operations. These sequences are called *machine cycles.* The decode circuit will also cause the computer to enter the correct cycle for a particular instruction.

Two registers are associated with the A.L.U. They are the ACCUMULATOR and REGISTER B. These two registers receive the values, binary numbers, which are to be operated on by the A.L.U. The accumulator is particularly significant to the A.L.U. operation because the result of the operation is placed in that register replacing the original contents. Figure 2.5 illustrates the A.L.U. arrangement.

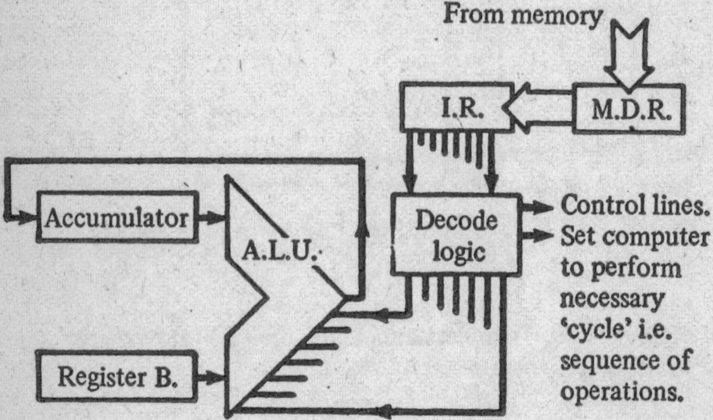

Fig. 2.5 *The instruction is transferred from the M.D.R. to the instruction register. The decode circuit configures the A.L.U. accordingly and sets the correct machine cycle.*

Instruction Formats

Now it is possible to deal with the problem of where the numbers come from. At least we know where the A.L.U. will get them from, the Accumulator and Register B. The truth is that most instructions, including incidentally our old friend ADD, only require one number. This is because the instructions refer to the Accumulator. For instance, the instruction ADD means add a number to the contents of the Accumulator, COMPARE means compare a number with the number already in the Accumulator. So only one number needs to be found, this is called the OPERAND. Most microprocessors operate in this way and are referred to as *accumulator oriented* devices.

It would be convenient and economical if we could embed the operand in the instruction word so that in one movement the A.L.U. could be told to ADD, and get the number to be added to the Accumulator. Well, we will see later that the technique of splitting the 8 bit instruction word into 'fields' is employed. But it would not really be practical to have, say, a 4 bit field for the actual operand, for two reasons. Firstly the number values which could be specified would be restricted to 0 to $(2^4 - 1)$ ie 0 to 15_{10}. Secondly, the four remaining bits would limit the number of alternative instructions which could use this instruction word format. For instructions of this sort, which require a number, the number is placed in the memory location following the location which contains the instruction. Remembering that the DECODE CIRCUIT sets the computer into a particular 'cycle' of operation it is easy to understand that the ADD cycle will involve two references to memory, one to get the instruction and another to get the OPERAND. A TWO BYTE INSTRUCTION. The process is illustrated by Figure 2.6.

All that remains to be done by the A.L.U. is to execute the instruction. In the case of ADD it would be to add the contents of Register B to the contents of the Accumulator.

A complete '2 byte' type of instruction has been followed through. Other types of instruction are also possible, as we shall see, involving various forms of machine cycle. This one example however has established the most fundamental principle on which the machine works, that is a FETCH and EXECUTE cycle. The computer is organised by its design to automatically and continually perform repeated FETCH and EXECUTE cycles, moving down the "page" of instructions

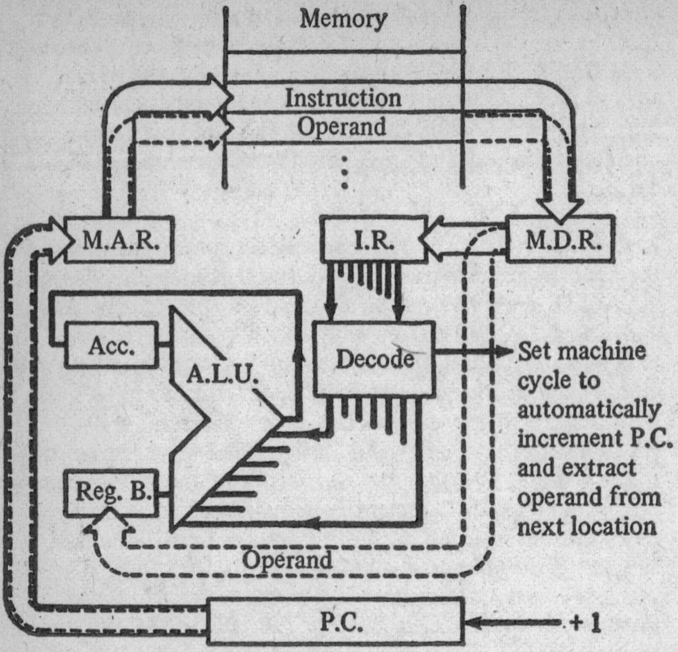

Fig. 2.6 The fetching of instruction and operand from two successive memory locations. A "two-byte instruction".

until it comes to one which says HALT. The complete set of instructions which can be used by a particular microprocessor, or computer, is known as THE INSTRUCTION SET*.

Although the architecture of a computer is a credit to man's genius, it is apparent that they are very slavish in their operation. There is certainly nothing to fear from a computer – unless we allow a fiend to program one!

General Purpose Registers
Included in the C.P.U. or microprocessor are a number of general purpose registers which are included to considerably

increase the number of instructions which the computer can perform. Also to provide various ways of addressing memory other than by the rather limited method of the Program Counter. Just to set us thinking, let's pose the question "What if the operand is held in a location which does not follow the instruction?" General purpose registers can also be used to store intermediate results in a calculation and for this reason the registers are sometimes referred to as 'Scratch Pad'.

Apart from speed of operation the thing which distinguishes these registers from locations in the memory is the fact that they can be used by the programmer in various ways by a single instruction. In other words their methods of use are a part of the instruction set.

The bit pattern of an 8 bit instruction can be made up of two or more 'fields'. For instance, the Zilog Z80 device includes in its instruction set an instruction word having three fields, as shown by figure 2.7.

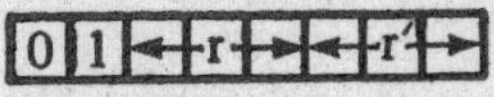

Fig. 2.7 An instruction having three fields.

This instruction means to the Z80, load the contents of r′ into r where r′ and r are any of the general purpose registers. The contents of r′ is the *source operand* and the contents of r is the *destination operand*. This instruction in effect transfers the binary number in r′ to r. The general purpose registers are identified by letters and each has a 3 bit code for use in the instruction word. The code for each register is shown in the table below.

A	=	1 1 1
B	=	0 0 0
C	=	0 0 1
D	=	0 1 0
E	=	0 1 1
H	=	1 0 0
L	=	1 0 1

Thus to transfer the contents of register C to register E the instruction word bit pattern would be as shown in fig. 2.8.

0	1	0	1	1	0	0	1

Fig. 2.8 Transfer contents of register C to register E.

The Digital Electronic Corporation (D.E.C.), LSI 11 micro-computer employs a 16 bit instruction word. As might be expected, this leads to a greater number of possibilities for the instruction word. The sixteen bits are subdivided into two fields as shown by fig. 2.9.

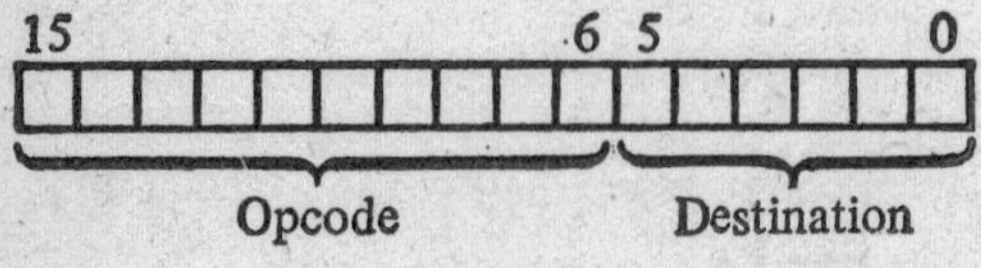

Fig. 2.9 A 16-bit instruction word format.

The destination field is further subdivided into two three-bit fields. Bits 0, 1 and 2 indicate one of the general purpose registers. Bits 3, 4 and 5 indicate the type, or 'mode', of addressing which is to be employed.

This table on page 35 shows that the B register may in fact be just one of several registers which could supply the A.L.U. with a second operand.

The INCREMENT instruction adds 1 to a specified register contents, or adds 1 to the contents of a memory location whose address is contained in the specified register, or adds 1 to some other location. Which of these three possibilities is actually implemented will be determined by the addressing mode set in bits 3, 4 and 5.

For REGISTER ADDRESSING the mode is 0. The full instruction for incrementing the contents of a register is obtained from the manufacturer's literature. The instruction word is shown below in Octal Coding, which is the coding used by the Digital Equipment Corporation.

Increment Instruction = 0 5 2 D D

where D D represents the addressing mode and the specified register.

The full instruction word to increment register number 2 is shown below in fig. 2.10.

	0	0	0	0	1	0	1	0	1	0	0	0	0	0	1	0
Octal code	0		5			2			0			2				

Fig. 2.10 16-bit instruction word for incrementing the contents of general purpose register No. 2.

From our earlier comments about the desirability of having 16 bits for addressing there must clearly be an advantage in having 16 bit general purpose registers. However, device manufacturers try, (and usually succeed), to anticipate all likely requirements. Most 8 bit devices have therefore been designed so that some of the 8 bit general purpose registers can be operated in pairs to make a total of 16 bits. This is particularly important in allowing pairs of general purpose registers to be employed as an additional program counter, or point to the location of an operand.

Intel 8080

The registers A – L are given a 3-bit code as shown in the table on page 38. The register pairing and a corresponding 2-bit identifying code (R.P.) are also shown for the 8080 device.

The instruction word format for subtracting 1 from the contents of a <u>pair</u> of registers is shown in fig. 2.11. The process of subtracting 1 is effectively to count backwards and known as *decrementing.*

A = 1 1 1
B = 0 0 0
C = 0 0 1
D = 0 1 0
E = 0 1 1
H = 1 0 0
L = 1 0 1

R.P. Code	Register pair
0 0	B – C
0 1	D – E
1 0	H – L

0	0	R	P	1	0	1	1

Fig. 2.11 The instruction word for decrementing the contents of a pair of registers by 1.

The full code to decrement register pair H – L would be as shown in fig. 2.12.

0	0	1	0	1	0	1	1

Fig. 2.12 Decrement register pair H – L.

These examples are deliberately taken from the instruction sets of different devices to show that the use of a bit-pattern to represent an instruction is common to all microprocessors. In fact this is true for all digital computers, large and small.

Addressing Modes

Some instruction bit patterns will contain a few bits, say a 3-bit field, to indicate the manner in which the operand is to be obtained. There are several ways this can be done, but by way of example we will consider one case at this point to establish the principle.

It has been shown how a 2-byte instruction can contain the instruction in the first byte, and the operand in the second byte. A three-byte instruction is also possible in which the second two bytes are understood by the computer to represent the two 8-bit bytes of a 16-bit address where the operand will be found. The computer will automatically enter the proper machine cycle to organise the extraction from memory of the operand, through the decoding of the bits which make up the addressing mode field. The addressing modes used in this example are referred to as IMMEDIATE and DIRECT respectively.

IMMEDIATE MODE:	The instruction contains the operand (2-byte instruction)
DIRECT:	The instruction (3-byte) contains the address of the operand.

Other common addressing modes are as follows:

REGISTER :	The instruction word contains a field which is coded to indicate a general purpose register in which the operand is located.
REGISTER INDIRECT:	The instruction contains a code to indicate a register (or register pair in the case of an 8-bit machine) which contains the address in memory where the operand is located. The register acts as a pointer to memory.

These addressing modes are typical of 8-bit microprocessors such as the Intel 8080. More powerful minicomputers and the advanced generation of microprocessors now being released (Intel 8086 and Motorola 6809) have many more sophisticated addressing modes. As pointed out in the introduction, intimate knowledge and understanding of a device, or system, must come from prolonged real experience. In this situation the manufacturer's literature must be the constant reference — at least for a week or two!

This chapter dealing with microprocessor and computer architecture is summarised by the block diagram of fig. 2.13. To allow the programmer to employ certain common pro-

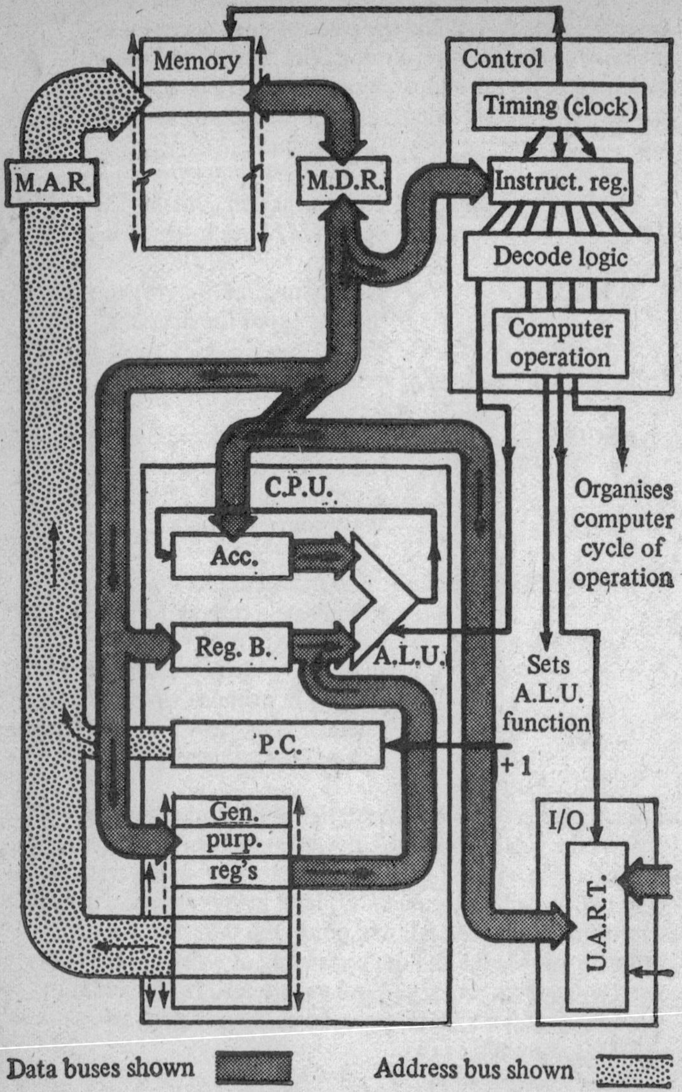

Fig. 2.13 Basic 8-bit microprocessor and computer architecture.

gramming techniques, and to provide useful engineering facilities some additions can be made to the system outlined so far. Fig 2.13 block diagram must therefore be regarded as basic.

The U.A.R.T. device shown in the I/O section is discussed further in chapter 3.

CHAPTER 3

PROGRAMMING

It has been firmly established in chapters 1 and 2 that computers operate using two-state devices. The two states 0 and 1 represent the computer's alphabet. If a language was based on just two letters like A and B then, neglecting the fact that some words would be impossible to pronounce clearly like AAAABBA, we could generate a vocabulary of sorts. In a similar way then the 1's and 0's form 'words' which have meaning for the computer and these patterns of 1's and 0's represent the MACHINE LANGUAGE. As we have seen, however, we must build into the operation of the computer a means by which it can distinguish between words and numbers, i.e. instructions and operands. Providing the machine language is known a program can be written and placed in the memory for the computer to follow. The problem is to know the language. Again the importance of the manufacturer's literature must be stressed. It was the manufacturer who devised the operation of the device, or computer, so only he can tell you of what its "instruction set" consists.

We can best understand the idea of machine language programming by a simple program example. The technique is exactly the same for complicated programs, they just take longer to write, and execute!

Program example 1. Using Intel 8080 device.

To add two numbers stored in two memory locations and store the result in a third specified memory location.

We will firstly collect all the information we will require.

Where is the program to be placed in memory? It is a good question. We will let it start at location 0_{10}.

Where will the two numbers to be added reside in the

memory?

Well of course they may be anywhere in the memory for one reason or another, but for this example we will just place them somewhere. The program we know is not a lengthy one, and we don't need to worry about 'bumping' into other programs in the memory, so we will need about 20_{10} locations for our adding program and therefore we can safely place the two numbers in locations 25_{10} and 30_{10}.

Where is the result to be placed?

We will choose location 5000_{10}, assuming at least this amount of memory is available to us.

What are the two numbers to be?

Let's keep it simple, say 63_{10} and 75_{10}.

All the addresses and values have been given in decimal and we know that this is not going to be very convenient so we had better convert them all to hexadecimal since this is the coding adopted by Intel and it will allow easy conversion to the 8 bit binary machine language when necessary, the addresses however will be 16 bits.

Decimal value	Hexadecimal value	
0	0 0 0 0	16 bit addresses
2 0	0 0 1 4	
2 5	0 0 1 9	
3 0	0 0 1 E	
5 0 0 0	1 3 8 8	
6 3	3 F	8 bit operands
7 5	4 B	

A useful exercise about this time in the production of a program is to draw up a MEMORY MAP. This is a diagramatic representation of the memory showing where the various blocks, or pieces of data will reside.

The memory map for this example is shown in fig. 3.1.

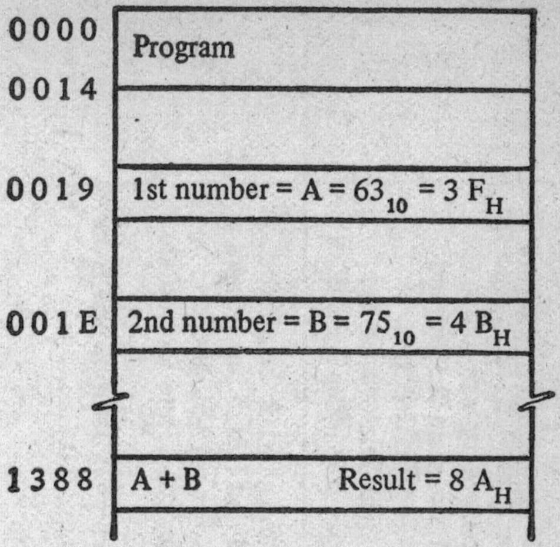

Fig. 3.1 The memory map.

Notice that the two operands (the data) are remote from the program. From this we know that we will not employ IMMEDIATE MODE addressing with 2-byte instructions.

The program

Instruction	Description	Machine language (HEX)
1. Load Accumulator Direct byte 1 | 3 A_H byte 2 | low order address byte 3 | high order address	This is a 3-byte instruction. Byte 1 is the instruction to move the contents of a memory location to the accumulator. Bytes 2 and 3 contain the low and high bytes of the memory location address. To put the 63_{10} into the accumulator then the address $0\ 0\ 1\ 9_H$ will be put into bytes 2 and 3.	3 A 1 9 0 0
2. Load Register Pair Immediate byte 1 | RP 1 byte 2 | low order data byte 3 | high order data where RP is the code for a specified register pair. In this case H and L; RP is therefore 10 as shown on page 38.	This is a 3-byte instruction. Byte 1 is the instruction to load the register pair H and L with the 3rd and 2nd byte respectively to form a 16-bit address. We are going to use register pair H and L to obtain the second number 75_{10}. H will be loaded with the high order byte and L the low order byte of the address $0\ 0\ 1\ E_H$.	2 1 1 E 0 0

Instruction	Description	Machine language (HEX)
3. Add Memory byte 1 | 8 6	This is a single byte instruction. The instruction is to add the contents of the memory location whose address is contained in register pair H L to the contents of the accumulator.	8 6
4. Store Accumulator Direct byte 1 | 3 2 byte 2 | low order address byte 3 | high order address	This is a 3 byte instruction. Byte 1 is the instruction to move the contents of the accumulator to the address contained in the second and third bytes.	3 2 8 8 1 3
5. Halt byte 1 | 7 6	This is a single byte instruction. The instruction stops the C.P.U.	7 6

The program is now complete and is seen to involve five instructions from the 8080 instruction set. The five instructions use a total of eleven memory locations.

For completeness the program is shown in fig. 3.2 as it would appear in the memory

0000	0 0 1 1 1 0 1 0
0001	0 0 0 1 1 0 0 1
0002	0 0 0 0 0 0 0 0
0003	0 0 1 0 0 0 0 1
0004	0 0 0 1 1 1 1 0
0005	0 0 0 0 0 0 0 0
0006	1 0 0 0 0 1 1 0
0007	0 0 1 1 0 0 1 0
0008	1 0 0 0 1 0 0 0
0009	0 0 0 1 0 0 1 1
000A	0 1 1 1 0 1 1 0
	⋮

Fig. 3.2 *The eleven-byte program in machine language as stored in the memory.*

Running the program is simplified by having it start at location zero. This is because the micro-computer is likely to have a RESET key or button which when operated will set the contents of the program counter to zero. If we had started the program at any other location it would have been necessary to initially load the program counter with the starting address before pressing the RUN switch.

All the instructions of example program 1 have been shown in hexadecimal coding. Many Single Board Development Computers (S.B.C.) incorporate a hexadecimal keypad. The operator in this case can enter data in hexadecimal and the keyboard will electronically convert each entry to binary for actual presentation to the memory, or processor. A set of binary coded lamps, or a series of alpha-numeric displays may be provided to show each address and its contents in hexadecimal. Simple systems of this sort are cheap and ideal for learning situations. The situation is rather like the scooter buyer who is very soon looking longingly at 750cc motor-cycles.

In addition to the RESET and RUN keys the basic computer will have a LOAD key. After setting the binary data by pressing the hexadecimal keys, the LOAD button is pressed to cause the data to be entered into the memory. Addressing each location is not usually necessary when loading the program because the program counter will be automatically advanced by 1, (i.e. incremented), after loading each byte of data.

Some micro, or minicomputers, have a set of keys on the front panel for entering data. The up position representing 0, the down position 1. The keys can be set to represent an address and the P.C. loaded by pressing the load address button. The data to be loaded to the location addressed is then set on the keys and the ENTER button pressed. In this way a program and data can be entered manually. This would be a very tedious way to enter a long program. A more advanced system is therefore certain to have a full keyboard interface, and V.D.U. or printer. There will additionally be a 'resident' program known as a *monitor* program which will recognise certain *command* instructions and perform the necessary operations. Two such commands may be GO and EXECUTE. 'GO' would be followed by an address in HEX code. When the EXECUTE key is pressed, or EX typed on the keyboard, the program will be run from the GO address.

The first programming example does not involve the entire instruction set but it does establish the principle upon which all programs are based. As pointed out earlier in chapter two, some of the instructions available in the instruction set are provided to allow the use of common programming techniques. This book is an introduction to computing and a fuller discussion of programming, and the necessary hardware organisation must be left to further reading. A few more instructions can be dealt with however and used in a second example program.

This program will determine the sum of three numbers entered into a 'datablock' in memory and enter the 2's C of this sum in a specified location.

The program structure will be as follows :–

1. Enter the values to be summed into a selected area of memory.

2. Set a 'pointer' to the 1st location of the datablock.

3. Set the accumulator contents to zero.

4. Add the contents of the location addressed by the pointer to the accumulator.

5. Increment the 'pointer'.

6. Repeat (4) and (5).

7. Repeat (4) and (5).

8. Complement the sum now held in the accumulator.

9. Add 1 to the contents of the accumulator.

10. Store the contents of the accumulator in the specified location.

11. Halt.

The data block in this case will consist of just three locations. We will let these be 5000_{10}, 5001_{10}, 5002_{10}. A register pair can be used to "point" to the locations in the data block. We will again choose to use register pair H – L. This "pointer" can be incremented to step through the data for successive additions.

Finally, the sum in the accumulator is complemented using an available instruction, 1 added to give the two's complement and this stored in memory. We will specify location 100_{10}.

The memory map is shown in fig. 3.3. (addresses are shown in decimal).

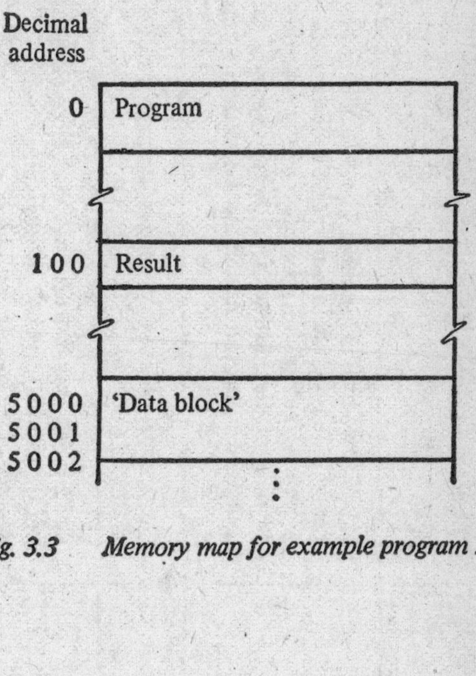

Fig. 3.3 Memory map for example program 2.

Example program 2

Instruction	Description	HEX CODE
Load Register Pair immediate	This instruction was explained in example program 1.	2 1 8 8 1 3
Move Immediate byte 1 | 0 0 D D D 1 1 0 byte 2 | 8 bit data In this case D D D is 1 1 1 – see page 38	This is a two-byte instruction. The data held in the second byte is moved into the register designated in byte 1. The register is indicated by the code in the three bit field marked D D D. The register is the accumulator (register A) and the data is 0.	3 E 0 0
Add Memory	This instruction was explained in example program 1.	8 6
Increment Register Pair 0 0 R P 0 0 1 1 R P = 1 0 for H-L see page 38.	This is a one-byte instruction. The content of the register pair indicated by the two bit code RP is incremented by one.	2 3

Instruction	Description	HEX CODE
	Repeat (4) and (5)	8 6
		2 3
	Repeat (4) and (5)	8 6
		2 3
Complement the Accumulator	A one-byte instruction. The content of the accumulator is complemented.	2 F
Increment Register 0 0 D D D 1 0 0 In this case D D D is 1 1 1	The content of register indicated by the code in the three bit field marked D D D is incremented by 1.	3 C
Store Accumulator Direct	Explained in example program 1. The memory address in this case is to be 100_{10}, i.e. 1100100_2, or 0064_H	3 2
		6 4
		0 0
Halt		7 6

The first five bytes of this program are used to prepare certain computer registers for the execution of the program. This process of preparation is often necessary and is known as *initialisation*. To keep the record straight it should be stated that Example Program 2 could be performed in a more elegant fashion but following the program given serves its purpose as an introductory exercise.

The collective name given to programs, programming techniques and special routines is SOFTWARE. The actual memory devices in which software (programs) are stored is nowadays being referred to as *firmware* something which lies between software and the electronic *hardware*.

In a microcomputer development system* which includes relatively large amounts of memory, and of course in large main frame computers, it is possible to have a program in the memory which will convert simplified instructions into the appropriate machine language. These converting programs allow the program to be more easily written in a HIGH LEVEL LANGUAGE. In effect it means that a single instruction can be written which might represent many bytes of machine language. A higher level language will also allow such things as *labels* to be used. Two quantities which may take on various values could be designated A and B by the statement :–

Let A = 7 2
Let B = 6 5

where the values 72 and 65 are decimal . . . there's an improvement! Another statement might then be:– (A + B) ↑ 3.5 . which means "raise the sum of A and B to the power 3.5". The high level language *compiler* will do all the conversion to the machine language for which the compiler is written. "Compiler" is simply the name given to the high level language converting program, which will require between 8k and 24k locations of memory depending upon the facilities offered and the language. A compiler will examine the high level language program statements as written by the programmer, known as the *source code*, and by reference to its *library* of programs, and tables, will re-write the program in the machine language of the computer. This final machine language form of the original program is known as the *object code*.

Several high level languages are in popular use, examples are BASIC, FORTRAN and COBOL. Each one has characteristics which make it most suitable for certain applications. FORTRAN is used mainly in engineering and science. COBOL in commerce. BASIC is perhaps the most popular and widely used language. A computer organised to receive

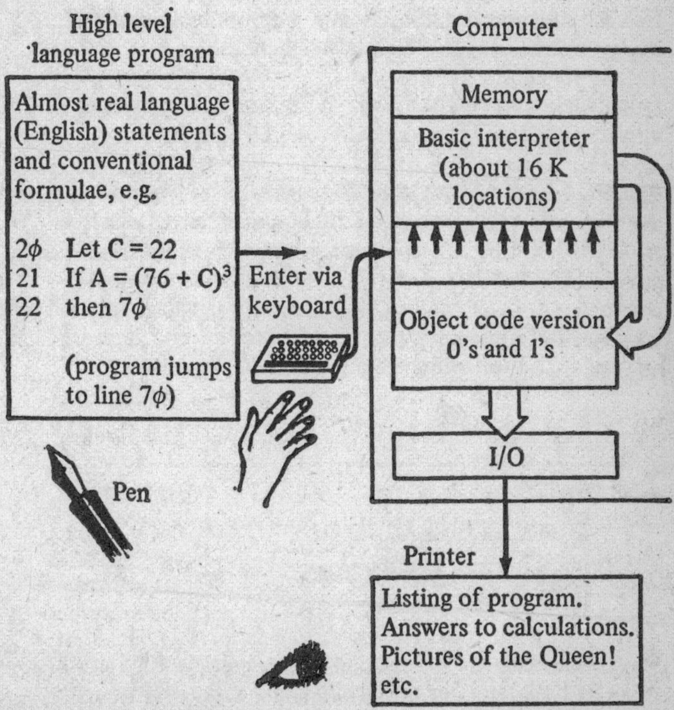

Fig. 3.4 The high level language programming process.

BASIC programs create the object code in memory as it receives each statement. The compiler for other high level languages creates, or compiles, the object code after receiving the entire source code program. This fundamental difference in operation leads to a BASIC compiling program to be referred to as an *interpreter*. This step by step treatment of the source code makes BASIC very suitable for time sharing which allows several users at separate keyboard terminals to share the computer. BASIC is also an easy language to learn whilst still offering powerful programming facilities.. Facilities such as sine, cosine and tangent tables, multiply, divide etc, For these reasons BASIC is well suited to educational situations.

Fig. 3.4 illustrates the function of a computer capable of being programmed in a high level language.

Other high level languages which find use in engineering applications are PL/M, PASCAL, and CORAL.

A limited form of high level language which is found extremely useful for development of microcomputer* programs is ASSEMBLY. The converting program in this case is known as an ASSEMBLER. Most manufacturers have developed assemblers for their device. The assembly language is based on a form of mnemonic shorthand which approaches real language. The following are a few familiar examples:

Instruction	Mnemonic
HALT	HLT
COMPLEMENT ACCUMULATOR	CMA
INCREMENT REGISTER PAIR B–C	INX 00

Program writing is thus enormously simplified. An assembler will also have facilities for labelling and some limited arithmetic processes. The assembler will also include certain checking routines which will give the operator of the system an indication of programming errors. The process of finding errors in programs is known as "debugging."

The important feature of an assembly language is that each instruction has a one-to-one relationship with the instruction set of the microprocessor for which the assembler is written. In engineering applications this can be important. A compiler cannot always be guaranteed to produce the shortest possible program in object code.

In addition to Compilers and Assemblers a veritable arsenal of software weapons is available, Monitors, Executives, Interpreters, Editors, and so on. Two simple but important pieces of software are worth special mention here, the BOOTSTRAP LOADER, and the ABSOLUTE LOADER. To appreciate the significance of these programs, and deal with a few questions which have probably arisen, we should take a look at *peripherals*.

"Peripherals" is a term used to describe all the equipments which surround the computer. Printers* onto which the computer can print programs, messages, and of course program results. Video Display Units (V.D.U.s)* which are an alternative to a printer but do not give a permanent copy. Bulk storage devices like magnetic tape and disk machines* on which large programs, or large quantities of data can be stored. Perhaps the most common piece of peripheral equipment is the TELETYPEWRITER (T.T.Y.) This incorporates a keyboard, printer, paper tape punch and paper tape reader.

It is the teletypewriter which we will use to explain how the program and data is entered into a computer. The keyboard, in addition to operating the printer like a conventional typewriter, provides an ASCII coded serial output signal corresponding to each available key. This serial output is fed to the computer 1/0 interface circuit. The interface will incorporate a U.A.R.T. which will convert the signal to parallel form for presentation to the computer data bus. Signals can similarly be sent in the opposite direction from the computer to operate the printer, or tape punch. The interface (U.A.R.T.)

will require control from the computer to ensure (a) a complete character is available in the U.A.R.T., (b) to program the U.A.R.T. to operate in the desired direction, (c) to deliver the coded signal when the computer is able to receive. The situation is illustrated by Fig. 3.5.

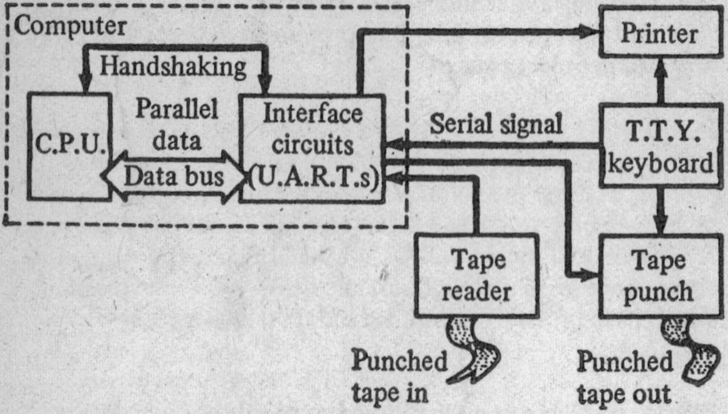

Fig. 3.5 T.T.Y. interface.

The keyboard can also be used to operate a paper-tape punch which punches holes across the tape to represent the A.S.C.I.I. code for each keyboard symbol. Fig 3.6 shows a section of punched tape.

The computer can also be caused to operate this tape punch, so a program could be punched directly from the keyboard or punched by the computer. This latter process is the way in which an assembler would deliver to us the program in machine language. It would then be necessary for us to feed the machine language version into the computer memory. For this we would use the tape-reader. The original assembler program could also be held on paper tape and this too would be initially supplied to the computer by use of the tape reader. The assembler, however, is a long program and could take about 20 minutes on a conventional tape reader to feed this into the computer. Magnetic tape, or disk, is therefore more convenient because it can operate faster, and store large programs more conveniently.

A key on the teletypewriter could be operated at any time. It is possible that the C.P.U. will be "busy" at this instant. Clearly the C.P.U. must be given warning that a character is to be sent. In other words the keyboard must request use of the C.P.U. The use of the C.P.U. in this random time fashion is made possible by an *interrupt* facility, provided by all self-respecting microprocessors. A signal applied to the INTERRUPT PIN of the microprocessor causes the C.P.U. to complete the instruction which it is currently performing, store the contents of the program counter and other internal registers, and turn its attention to the interrupting device. It does this by entering an *interrupt service routine* which is simply a small program written specifically to deal with the requirements of the interrupting device. At the completion of the interrupt service routine the C.P.U. program counter, and other registers are re-loaded (remember they were stored) and the original program continues.

The program counter, and internal register contents are stored in a specified area of memory known as a *stack*. A Register, which acts like a program counter, known as the *stack pointer*

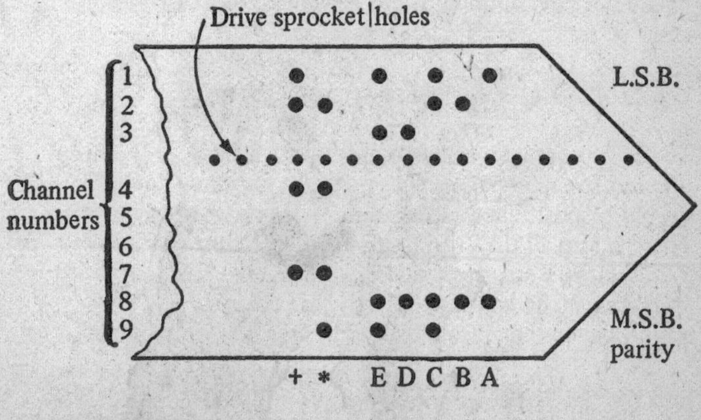

Fig. 3.6 A section of A.S.C.I.I. coded punch tape.

(S.P.), is used to address the stack area of memory. (see PUSH and POP).

The interrupt is also extremely valuable in engineering applications. A microprocessor can in fact respond to several different interrupting sources. A separate interrupt service routine being available in memory for each source. A special I.C. device is required for organising several interrupts to the microprocessor.

It is not sufficient to simply press the lift button in a hotel. One must also wait for the lift to arrive and the doors to open. Similarly it is not sufficient to simply apply a signal to the interrupt pin. The interrupting device must also wait for the C.P.U. to become ready before sending the character, or data. When the C.P.U. is ready to receive data it issues an *interrupt acknowledge* signal to the source of the interrupt. On receipt of this signal the source identifies itself in order that the C.P.U. can go for the correct interrupt service routine. The source may in fact identify itself by providing the starting address of its own interrupt service routine. This form of interrupt is known as a *vectored* interrupt.

The interchange of signals, interrupt request, and acknowledge, is just one example of how the C.P.U. and other peripheral devices communicate. The general term used to describe this is very apt, *handshaking*.

Fig. 3.7 illustrates the basic interrupt operation.

To put a program into a computer whose memory is empty requires some organisation as might be expected. Where it should be positioned in the memory is one obvious question. There is also all the organisation of the memory for programs with several parts, and identifying the beginning and end of each character. At last we have a use for the Bootstrap Loader and Absolute Loader, previously mentioned.

The loading program is the means by which all this organisation is accomplished. The complete loading program is there-

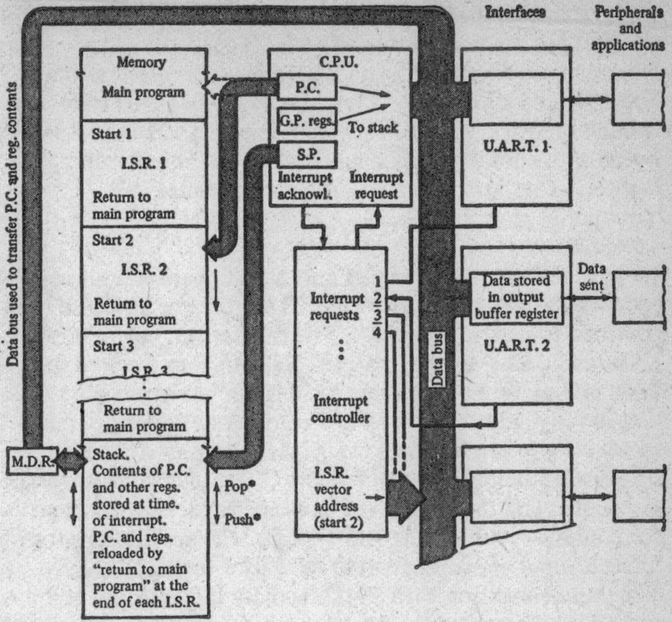

Fig. 3.7 A simplified view of the vectored interrupt process allowing several levels of interrupt.

fore not small. But we still have the problem of getting this loading program into the memory. The loader is arranged in two parts. First the Bootstrap Loader which is only a few bytes in length. This may be put into the computer manually using the front panel keys. This small program is then used to organise the loading of the Absolute Loader from paper tape. The Absolute Loader can now be used to 'suck in' the more complicated user programs, assemblers or compilers.

A more usual, and certainly more convenient, way to have a loader program is to contain it in R.O.M*. In this way panel keys are not necessary and the loader R.O.M. sits in the computer and ready immediately at switch-on. In fact nowadays even the simplest of systems can contain other program facilities in R.O.M. (The monitor mentioned earlier). For example the program to organise a hex coded keypad, or even full keyboard and V.D.U. Other programs contained in the R.O.M. could allow use of a few simple COMMAND statements to move a block of data from one part of the R.A.M. memory to another, or examine the contents of all internal registers. This latter feature is of great assistance in 'debugging' programs.

We have used in two examples only a small part of a microprocessor's instruction repertoire. The programs have also been confined to machine language. The chapters on binary arithmetic and codes, and basic architecture are also devoted to basic principles. Each of these aspects can be expanded enormously, and they are all in a continuous state of development. New technologies allowing more complex devices to be manufactured. Development of existing high level language techniques and the creation of new languages. New concepts for computer architecture and systems. The applications for microcomputers is estimated to be tens of thousands each year. By comparison with all this activity this introduction may seem trivial. But the fundamental theory and principles do not change and they are vital to further understanding, particularly from an engineering point of view.

The reader is finally recommended to study the entries in the Glossary, in particular FLAGS, LOOP, JUMP which are an extension to the main text.

GLOSSARY

ACCESS TIME. The time interval between the instant at which the C.P.U. is instructed to fetch the contents of a memory location and the instant at which the contents are available for use in the C.P.U. (usually in the accumulator). There will be a similar time interval between the instant at which the C.P.U. is instructed to send a byte of data to memory and the instant at which it actually arrives at its destination in memory.

The maximum speed at which the C.P.U. is capable of working must clearly dictate the minimum access time. But the speed at which the memory, or bulk storage device, can operate, will clearly have an influence on the time to transfer data to and from the C.P.U. Peripheral devices, and semiconductor memory, have their own access time characteristic. In general bulk storage mediums such as floppy disc, magnetic tape, and paper tape are slow by comparison with any form of semiconductor memory.

BAUD. Commonly used to indicate the rate at which data is transmitted and refers to the bits per second (b.p.s). For example a V.D.U. might be described as being set to operate at 2,400 baud.

BISTABLE (Circuit). A circuit which has two stable states. As a 'discrete' circuit* this would consist of two transistors connected in such a way that either will conduct heavily when the other is switched off. The application of a pulse (trigger) will cause a changeover to take place, the conducting transistor

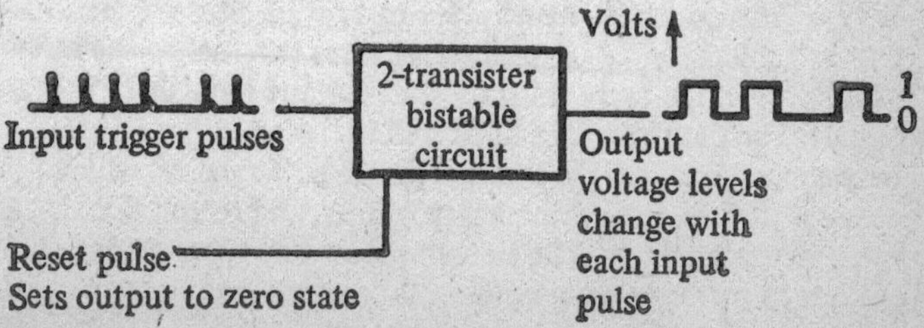

will be switched off and the non-conducting will be switched on. The circuit is also known more generally as a Flip-Flop. A high voltage or a low voltage is provided at the output, depending on the *state* in which the circuit is set. The circuit acts as a switch giving a "1 state" or a "0 state".

With circuit modifications several forms of bistable operation can be achieved. A bistable circuit which is set to the 1 state, or 0 state, by applying a 1 or 0 state to the input can be used as a memory cell.

BIT. An individual 1 or 0 state in a binary number or character code. A register consisting of eight bistable elements can store eight bits of data, an 8-bit register.

BULK STORAGE. A term used to describe peripherals which store large quantities of data. Magnetic-tape, paper-tape, and disc* storage are all examples of bulk storage, also known as "back up store".

Paper-tape, and magnetic-tape are most suitable for *sequential* storage. This means the tape running in one direction continually whilst data is deposited or extracted. It would not be very convenient to access the piece of data on the end of the tape which was on the inside of the full reel! Such a requirement would have an alarming effect on access time*.

For true *random access* (see MEMORY) operation for bulk storage it is necessary to use a disc storage medium. In this case the head can move, and the disc turn, to allow almost immediate access to any point on the disc surface.

BUS. The collective name given to a set of interconnections within a microprocessor, or a set of wires external to the microprocessor, which carry the data, address, and handshake* signals. The data bits are transferred in the microprocessor between registers on the internal data bus. The wires which connect devices and peripherals together, and to the C.P.U. form an external bus. The sixteen binary bits representing an address in memory are placed on the address bus by the program counter.

BYTE. The smallest part of a complete binary word which can be manipulated. Nowadays the word byte is used exclusively for eight bits. A sixteen bit word can be separated into two eight-bit bytes. Another term gaining popularity for four bits is *nibble*.

CASCADE. Normally used to describe a series of waterfalls – each one feeding into the next. In electronics the word has the same meaning, as for instance when amplifiers are cascaded, the output of one circuit feeds into the input of the next.

CHARACTER. The name used to describe a letter or symbol but is used in general to mean the coding pattern of any binary piece of information.

CLEAR. A program term used to indicate the setting of *flags**, and registers to the 0 state. An instruction "CLEAR REGISTER B" would set all eight bits of register B to 0.

CROSS ASSEMBLER. An assembler is a program usually resident in a development system which allows easier machine language programming for a particular microprocessor. The development system will usually be based upon the same microprocessor. However it is possible to have a cross assembler which is resident in a computer based on some other microprocessor. In fact a cross assembler is usually used in a main frame computer. Cross compilers also exist which allow a *target* microprocessor to be programmed with a high level language on a mainframe computer.

DEDICATED APPLICATION. Quite simply this means that a microprocessor, or computer, has been dedicated to a specific task. A microprocessor operated washing machine is an example of a dedicated application.

DEVELOPMENT SYSTEM. A development system is a computer and associated equipments on which programs for

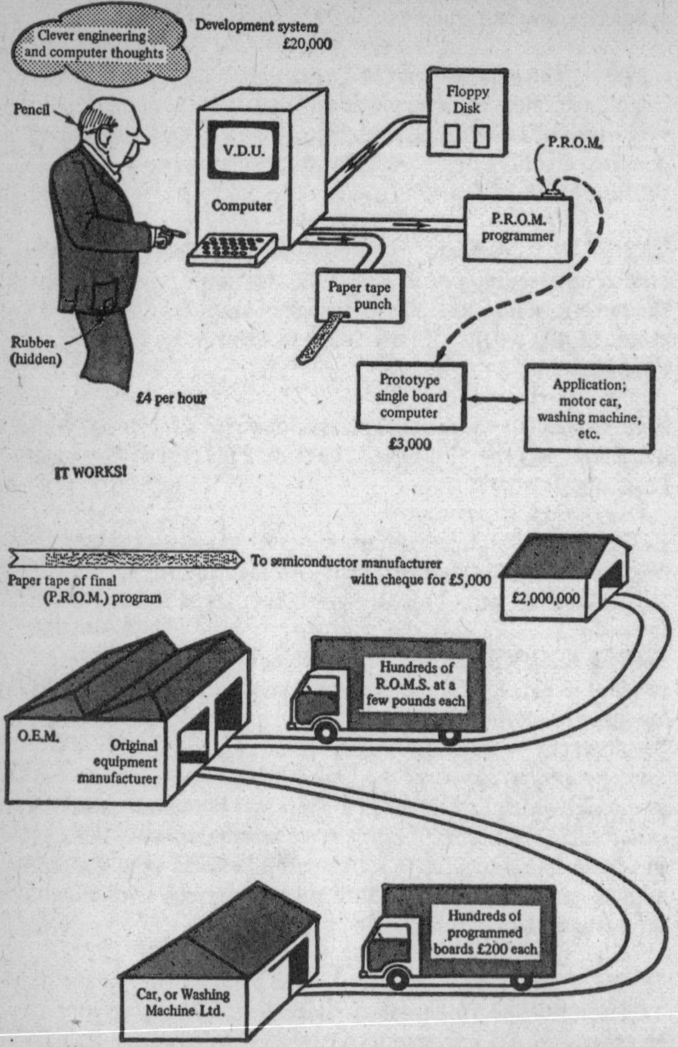

The development of a dedicated application for volume production. The costs shown are intended to give an indication and should not be taken as exact figures for all applications.

dedicated applications* can be developed and tested. The computer used in the development system, as might be expected, operate with the same instruction set* as the microprocessor which will be used in the final application. There are, however, systems usually referred to as *Laboratory Systems* which can be used to develop programs for a number of different microprocessors.

A V.D.U.* paper tape, and/or some form of magnetic bulk storage, and the inevitable keyboard is normally present in the system. The memory space will also be relatively large compared with the final application memory. This is necessary to store the armoury of *software tools* probably supplied by the computer device manufacturer. The software tools will include assembly language or high level language program (compiler)*, a *monitor program* to supervise the running of the system, and special routines like *editors* and *debug programs*. There are no prizes for guessing what this latter program does for the development engineer! The development and production sequence for a dedicated application is shown on page 66.

DISCRETE (Circuit). This indicates that a circuit has been constructed using transistors, resistors, capacitors etc. as separate components (*discrete* components), as compared with an *Integrated* Circuit.

DISK MACHINES. Disks with a magnetic oxide surface can be used to store the 1's and 0's of machine language. The *bits* of information are laid down on the surface, in concentric circles, as a magnetic dot. The data is deposited by a magnetic recording head which can also be used to detect the magnetic dots. In this way the head can be used to WRITE to memory or READ from memory.

The most usual form of disk used for microcomputer development systems* is a *floppy disk*. As the name suggests the disk used is flexible and can be loaded into the machine in a cassette type package. The basic principle is illustrated by the diagram below.

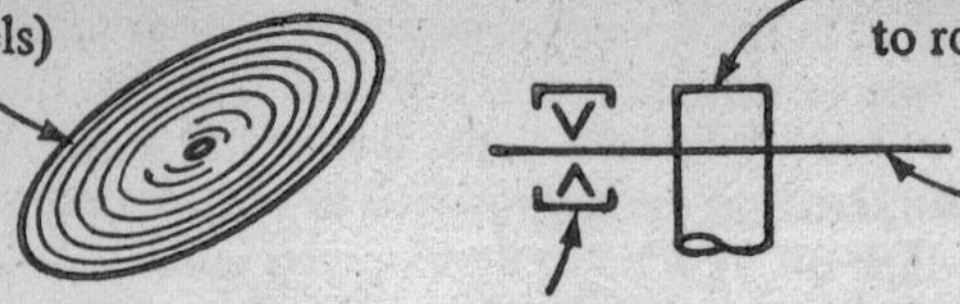

Typical Characteristics:

Total storage disk	:	100,000 characters
Speed (transfer rate)	:	5μseconds to extract one character.
cost	:	In excess of £2,000

D. M. A. Direct Memory Access. This is a programming technique which allows a single byte, or a block of bytes, from an external device to be entered directly in to the memory without use of the C.P.U. Without the involvement of the accumulator in the usual way this method of delivering data to memory is extremely fast.

ENABLE. Some electronic circuits are arranged to operate only at specific times, and only if certain other conditions are satisfied. A circuit to be operated in this way is provided with an *"enable"* which if set to the high logic level (a 1 state), allows the circuit to function. Notice the enabling signal does not itself operate the circuit. The safety switch on the door of a washing machine 'enables' the machine operation, but the 'start' button actually starts the machine.

FLAG. A bistable* circuit set to a 1 state to indicate that a particular operation has taken place. Some instructions in the instruction set of a microprocessor involve an examination, or testing, of certain *flags* which are set under various circumstances. Two common flags in microprocessors are:

1. The CARRY FLAG, set to 1 if the accumulator overflows. The carry bit.
2. ZERO FLAG, set to 1 if the result of an instruction sets the accumulator to zero.

Flags are discussed in detail in the appendix.

GATE. (see logic).

HANDSHAKE. A name given to the interchange of signals between C.P.U. and external devices, and peripherals, which establishes the correct time, and circumstances, for their operation. The operation usually involves the transfer of serial data on special lines or parallel data on the external bus lines.

HARDWARE. A term used to describe the circuit boards I.C.'s discrete components (if any), wire, cables, cabinets etc. as distinct from software*. There is a tendency nowadays to call memories *firmware* because although a R.O.M. memory is an I.C. it does contain software.

INSTRUCTION SET. The complete range of arithmetic, logic, memory addressing, and data manipulation, operations which a microprocessor, or computer, can perform without the aid of software. i.e. instructions in machine language* which the microprocessor can interpret and perform.

INTEGRATED CIRCUIT. This is a small square of silicon into which has been diffused many transistors, diodes, and resistors. The silicon chip or die will only be a few square millimetres in area and mounted in a plastic package with metal pins for connection to the circuit. Because such packages have these pins in two rows down opposite sides of the rectangular package these are referred to as 'dual-in-line'. (D.I.L.) Because of their appearance they are also sometimes called 'bugs' (American). Most microprocessors have 40 pins. The Texas Instrument microprocessor 9900 has 64 pins.

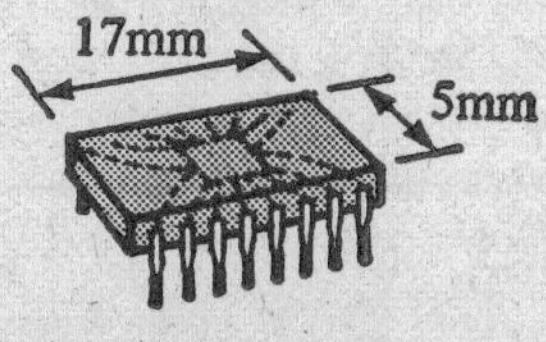

A conventional I.C. in Dual-in-line package.

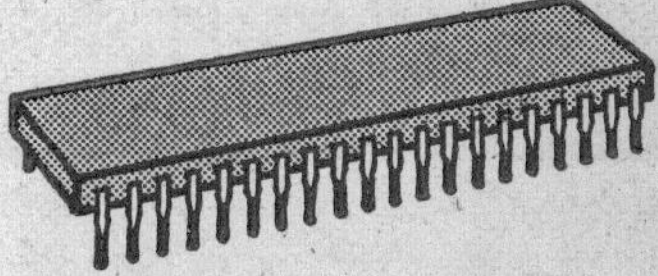

A typical microprocessor in a 40-pin dual-in-line package.

Other package forms are possible, 'cans' and 'flat packs' for instance. These forms are not employed for microprocessors.

One Intel Corporation Device, the 8086 microprocessor, contains 29,000 transistors on a chip of 225mils square.

Integrated circuits having a total number of components measured in hundreds are classified as *Medium Scale Integration* whereas devices having thousands of components are classified as *Large Scale Integration*, M.S.I. and L.S.I. respectively. Manufacturing techniques are now developed to produce devices with transistor counts of 10's of thousands, and has now lifted the state of the art to V.L.S.I.

So far as manufacturers are concerned their principle objectives in development of I.C.s include:—

Reduction of cost
Reduction of Power dissipation
Greater Packing Density (More transistors per chip)
Increased speed of operation
Single power supply operation
Reliability.

The situation is a 'Swings and Roundabouts', you can't have them all at once.

INTERFACE. This term is used to describe circuitry which lies between two units or sections. It would be nice to think that the computer (C.P.U. board) could be merely plugged in to any peripheral' device. Well, sometimes that is possible, but very often some *interfacing* is required. Even if we can plug them straight in it is probably because the two equipments contain input and output circuits for some form of standardised interfacing arrangement. (20 mA. loop, or RS 232 for example).

JUMP. A program instruction which causes the program to jump to a specified point in the program other than the next. The program can jump forward, or backwards. A *conditional* *jump* is a program jump which is made if a specific condition is satisfied. In a high level language BASIC such a jump may appear as :—

```
69 LET B = 12.
70 LET A = K↑2
71 IF  A = B
72 THEN 128
73 PRINT B
74 PRINT A
```

These four lines of program cause the program to jump to line number 1 2 8 if K^2 is equal to 12, where K is perhaps some constant evaluated earlier in the program. If this condition is not satisfied the program continues with line 73, 74 and onwards in the usual sequential manner.

In machine language for a microprocessor a conditional jump can be performed by using a COMPARE instruction and a JUMP IF NOT EQUAL, or JUMP IF EQUAL instruction. The COMPARE instruction subtracts the contents of a specified register from the accumulator and sets the Z flag to 1 if the contents are equal, ie the accumulator goes to Zero if they are equal. The JUMP IF EQUAL and JUMP IF NOT EQUAL instructions test the Z flag* and execute the instruction accordingly, either performing a program jump or continuing sequentially depending on whether the Z flag is set to 1 or 0.

A machine language program to cause a conditional jump using mnemonic notation and HEX code for the instructions is shown.

HEX	Mnemonic Instruction	Comment
8 A	A D C D	Adds the contents of register D to the accumulator.
B 8	C M P B	Compares the contents of register B with the contents of the accumulator by subtracting. The Z flag is set to 1 if the result is zero.
C 2	J N Z 32 AB	Tests the state of the Z flag and jumps to location $32AB_H$ for the next instruction if the Z flag is not set. If the Z flag is set to 1 then the program continues with the next sequential instruction.

LATCH. This is a hardware device which can hold a binary bit, or a complete character, for a period of time longer than the period for which the binary state(s) are applied to its input terminal(s). An 8-bit byte of data may be present on the data bus for only a few micro-seconds, or less, but the peripheral, or the computer, which is to receive the data may not be ready to receive at that time. The trick is to grab the data whilst it is there and lock it into a latch until such time as it can be used. The latch will need to be enabled* at the time the data is present. The diagram illustrates the latching action.

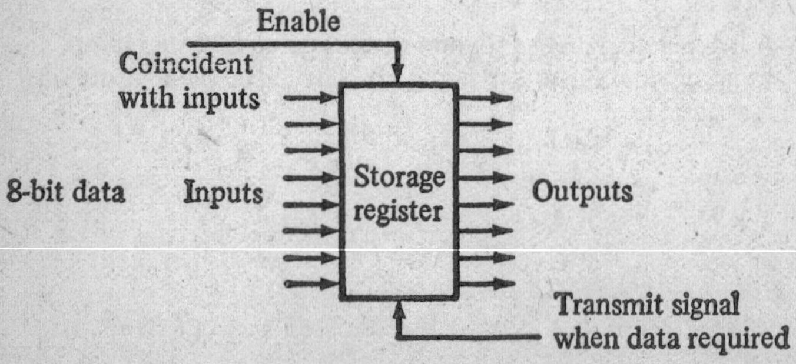

8-bit data latch.

L.E.D. LIGHT EMITTING DIODE. This is an electronic device which emits light when a potential is applied. That does not sound like a big deal, after all any torch bulb does that. But an L.E.D. is a *solid state* device, efficient and very reliable. Several colours are available.

LOGIC. This refers to circuits and devices designed to execute logic functions. The theory of logic is based on situations which have just two possibilities, such as yes, or no. The two possibilities are complements; that is to say, if one possibility exists then the other certainly does not. If children understood the idea of a *complement* it would not be necessary for mothers to say "When I say no, I do not mean yes." 'On' and 'Off' are also examples of complements. Logic theory represents these various complement conditions in a general way by 1 or 0. This idea is developed further in chapter 1. The basic *gate* circuits used to build up complex logic functions are as follows.

Inverter: a 1 state at the input generates a 0 state at the output, and vice versa. Where a 0 state is a low potential and a 1 state is a high potential such as 1 volt and 4 volt respectively. In effect it is possible to say that the output is not the input, hence the circuit is usually known as a NOT gate.

Symbol

A NOT gate.

In logic shorthand this can be expressed $F = \overline{A}$
The bar above A indicates that F is NOT A.
So if A = 1, F = 0, if A = 0, F = 1.
High voltage level in gives low voltage level out, or vice versa.

AND: This gate may have two or more inputs. A 1

state appears at the output when a 1 state exists at A and B and C and D etc. depending upon the number of inputs.

Symbol

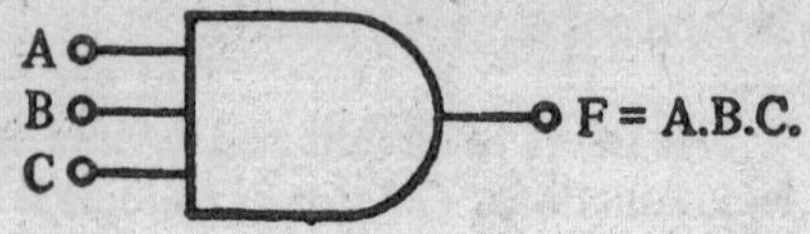

Three-input AND gate.

The shorthand notation uses a dot to indicate the AND function. F = A.B.C. means the output will be a 1 when A and B and C are 1. If this condition is not satisfied then the output will be a 0.

OR: Also a gate with two or more inputs but in this case the output will be a 1 state when the input at A or B or C or D etc. is a 1 state.

Symbol

Three-input OR gate.

The shorthand notation uses a 'plus' sign to indicate the OR function. Thus F = A + B + C.

The output is a 1 state when A or B or C is a 1 is easily seen to include the AND function. For this reason the gate condition shown here is described as an INCLUSIVE OR gate. It is, however, possible to arrange the circuitry to act in a total OR capacity by excluding the AND condition. In other words When A and B and C are each at the 1 state the output will be 0. Such a gate is known as an EXCLUSIVE OR gate.

NAND: This gate is an AND gate followed by a NOT gate

so that with the AND condition satisfied the output will NOT be the input, i.e. a 1 at A and B and C will give a 0 at the output.

Symbol

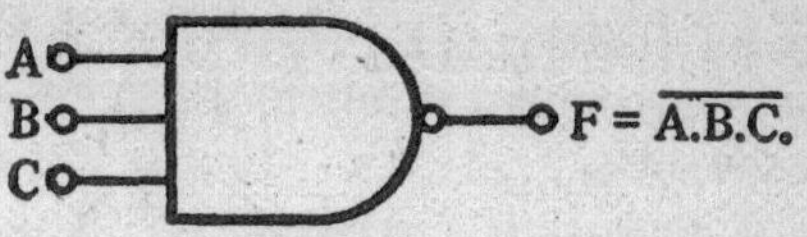

Three-input NAND gate.

NOR: This should not be too difficult to guess. Take no credit then if you realise that this must be an OR gate followed by a NOT.

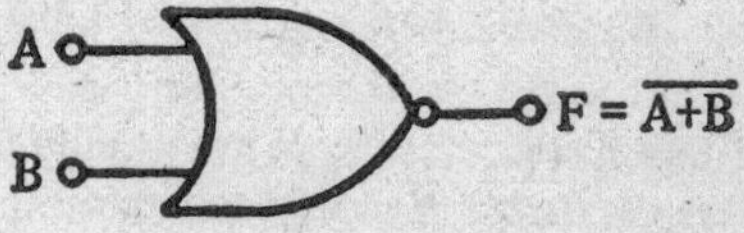

Input NOR gate.

By using combinations of gates complex logic fuctions can be set up.

A simple example: generate a signal to "enable"* a motor car starter-motor solenoid under the following conditions:

When (a) All four doors are closed.
(b) The bonnet is closed.
(c) The radiator is full of water.
(d) Adequate oil lies in the sump.
(e) Brake fluid is in the reservoir.
(f) The servicing override switch is operated.

It would seem obvious to use (a) - (e) as an AND function with (f) as an OR. Using our 'shorthand'

$$F = (a. b. c. d. e) + (f)$$

This shorthand used for the mathematics of logic is called Boolean Algebra. (The *Mathematical Analysis of Logic* by G. Boole was published in 1847 so this is not new!)

To form this function in hardware* is easy, but we can think of more complex situations which would require many more gates.

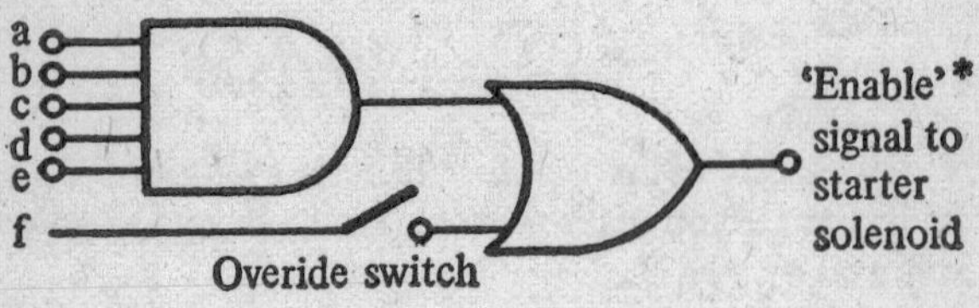

Gate circuit for (a. b. c. d. e.) + (f).

The logic fuctions discussed here are usually included in a microprocessor's *Instruction set** which means that a single microprocessor can replace large numbers of discrete logic gates, (or T.T.L.* logic packages). In fact the demand by users for 1.C.'s with ever increasing complexity which were not economical to produce in small numbers was the spur to manufacturers to create a device which could do anything any individual user required. "All things to all men" is the usual phrase to describe this. The enormous market for calculators generated the money and incentive to develop the necessary integrated circuit manufacturing techniques. So the microprocessor was a natural evolution so far as hardware was concerned. Having produced this device the designers and engineers at the user end were then required to 'program' the device to their needs. The greatest engineering effort was then switched from designing circuits with discrete components (or at best T.T.L.) and the manufacture of large numbers of printed circuit boards, to computer techniques or, in a word, 'software'*. The user end therefore experienced a REVOLUTION.

LOOP. A software term used to describe a programming

technique in which a section of a program is repeated a predetermined number of times. In other words the program loops back to a previous line, the loop formed being repeated if necessary a set number of times before continuing with the main program.

The sketch illustrates the idea of a loop in a program.

MACHINE LANGUAGE. The patterns of 1's and 0's which form the instructions understood by the computer, or microprocessor. A program written in this binary fashion is also said to be in 'machine code'.

MEMORY (Memories). A memory is a collection of bistable* *cells* arranged into groups of 8. Each cell can be set in the "1" state or the "0" state, thus each group of eight cells can store a pattern of 1's and 0's which can represent a number in binary form, or an instruction. Blocks of numbers or sequences of instructions, can thus be stored in consecutive memory locations, each location being a group of 8 cells.

The memory used with a microprocessor is required to have different characteristics for different applications and so various forms of memory exist.

R.A.M. Random Access Memory. This form of memory allows data to be placed in any location. (WRITE) or taken from any location (READ).

R.O.M. Read Only Memory. As the name suggests data can only be taken from this form of memory (READ ONLY). A manufacturer would therefore choose R.O.M. in which to store his washing machine control program for example. It would not do for a housewife to have access to the program . . . or would it? Perhaps that day will come. In the meantime we can expect manufacturers of computerised cars, washing machines, telephone answering machines, vending machines and petrol pumps to lock their programs firmly in R.O.M.

Producing R.O.M.s is in fact quite an expensive business so only large volume requirements are economical. It is, however, possible to have a form of R.O.M. which the user can program relatively easily and cheaply. This form is known as PROGRAMMABLE READ ONLY MEMORY, 'PROM'.

Just so that everyone gets what they want, or need, ERASABLE PROGRAMMABLE READ ONLY MEMORY, 'EPROM', is also manufactured. This allows a memory's contents to be erased and the memory used again. This is naturally very useful in development departments.

All these forms of memory are available as integrated circuits. An integrated circuit *memory chip* will typically contain 1K, 2K or 4K bits of storage. R.O.M.s and P.R.O.M.s are organised into 8-bit locations, but R.A.M. chips are organised in single bits. A R.A.M. chip may therefore be described as a 1K x 1 bit memory. Eight of these memory chips would be used to form 1K, 8-bit R.A.M. locations. The new Bubble memory, which employs magnetic "bubbles", will revolutionise the storage capacities of memory devices. (see SYMBOLS for explanation of K).

A microcomputer system could require RAM, ROM and PROM so the entire system's memory could be a mixture.

MICROCOMPUTER. A computer system based on an 8-bit microprocessor, usually with limited input/output facilities compared with larger more expensive systems. The memory size is probably also limited to a few K* bytes. A microcomputer may however be coupled to a floppy disc*. In this case the distinction between mini and micro becomes less distinct in terms of bulk storage. The two parameters which best define a microcomputer are cost and speed of operation (cycle time). A dedicated single board, or single chip computer must certainly be described as a microcomputer.

Systems based on the latest generation of fast execution time, 16-bit microprocessors with powerful instruction sets are now challenging the traditional minicomputer* for many business, and scientific applications.

Typical Instruction execute time 5-20μ* seconds.

Typical cost £200 – £600 excluding peripherals.

MINICOMPUTER. A 16-bit computer system having at least 8k memory, extensive interrupt facilities, and a more powerful instruction set than the average "workhorse" 8-bit microprocessor. Other advanced features are likely to be available such as, D.M.A.* and hardwired arithmetic. The electronics of the system will be certain to be contained on several different boards. A C.P.U. board, a memory board and an I/O board held in a 3-slot card-cage might be a minimum arrangement.

Minicomputers are now as powerful in computer terms as large mainframe computers of 10 years ago. This trend of micros to beat minis, and minis to beat main frame machines is a continuing one. Mainframe applications such as the organising of motor-car registrations can expect to become exceptional.

Typical Instruction execution time 400 n* seconds to 2μ seconds.

Typical cost £3,000 +. Excluding peripherals.

MODEM. A device which allows telephone lines (transmission lines) to be used for sending binary data to a remote point. Telephone lines are designed primarily to be used with alternating a.c. signals at a voice frequency around 3KHz (3,000 cycles). Binary coded data is represented by two d.c. voltage values, high = 1, and low = 0. It is therefore necessary to modulate an a.c. signal with the binary data if it is to be efficiently transmitted. This in effect means converting the d.c. voltages to a.c. The word MODEM is derived from modulator — demodulator. The instrument is basically a bed into which a telephone hand-set can be placed. The mouth piece is positioned over a microphone and the earpiece over a loud-speaker through which tone signals can be transmitted and received respectively. The idea is illustrated by the sketch.

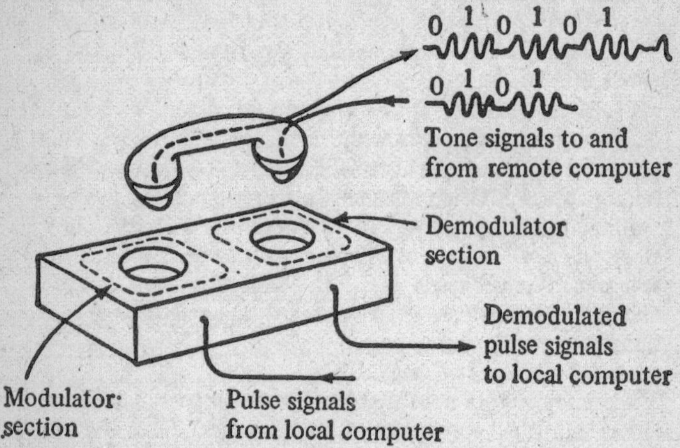

The Modem used for linking to a remote computer over a telephone line.

PERIPHERALS. A term used to refer collectively to all the external equipments commonly associated with a computer, such as printers and V.D.U's.

POP. A machine language program term to indicate the removal of a byte of data from the program *stack*. In effect this instruction causes the stack pointer (S.P.) to be decremented by 1. See page 37.

PRINTERS. Anyone who has watched the T.V. football results will have seen a 'printer' in operation. In this case it is used as a teleprinter, receiving the transmitted signals from a distance, but the idea is the same. Put simply, it is a remote controlled electric typewriter receiving signals for the charac-ters to be typed. The standard printer, such as that in a teletype machine (TTY) is relatively slow with a speed of 10 characters/sec. High speed printers, however, are available which print a complete line rather than a single character. The time saving allows printing up to 2000 lines/minute.

PUSH. A machine language program term to indicate the placing of a byte of data on the program *stack*. In effect this instruction causes the stackpointer to be incremented by 1.

R.A.M. See MEMORY.

REGISTERS. A series of memory *cells* used to contain an entire binary character. Each cell contains one *bit* of the information. See page 64.

R.O.M. See MEMORY.

SET. A program term used to indicate the setting of a flag*, or register bit to the 1 state.

SHIFT. The process of moving the bits contained in a register to the left or right, a '0' being brought into the vacated end bit. Most microprocessors have a SHIFT LEFT (S.L.) and SHIFT RIGHT (S.R.) instruction in their instruction set. An illustration of a shift right is shown.

| 1 | 0 | 1 | 0 | 1 | 0 | 1 | 1 | Before shift right

⟶

| 0 | 1 | 0 | 1 | 0 | 1 | 0 | 1 | After shift right.

SOFTWARE. A general term used usually to refer to computer programs, but sometimes extended to include literature.

SUBROUTINE. A program to perform a function which is required by a main program. This one program, usually shorter than the main program, can be used repeatedly by the main program as required. The main program jumps to the subroutine when directed by a JUMP instruction.

SYMBOLS. Although microelectronics, and microprocessors in particular, are relatively recent developments they are in fact developments of general electronics over many years. Consequently most of the symbols in use are traditional electrical and electronic symbols.

Hz	•	Hertz, a unit of frequency, previously referred to as *cycles per second*.
K kilo,	•	a thousand. Because memory is organised with locations numbered to the base 2 a 1K byte memory actually refers to 1024_{10} bytes. 2^{10}
L.S.B.	•	least significant bit.
L.S.I.	•	large scale integration
M mega,	•	a million.
m.p.u.	•	microprocessing unit.
M.S.B.	•	most significant bit.
M.S.I.,	•	medium scale integration.
n nano,	•	$\frac{1}{100,000,000}$ or 10^{-9}
o.e.m.	•	original equipment manufacturer.
T.T.Y.	•	Teletypewriter.
μ micro	•	$\frac{1}{1,000,000}$ or one millionth, 10^{-6}

TELETYPWRITER. (T.T.Y.) Also known simply as a *terminal*. This peripheral combines a keyboard, printer, papertape punch, and papertape reader.

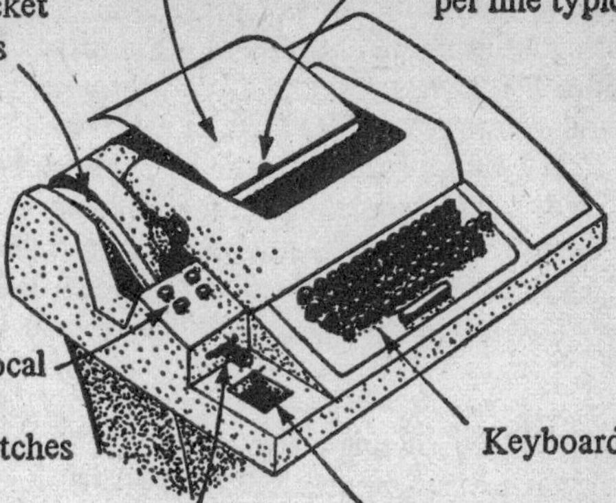

Typical teletypewriter terminal.

TRUTH TABLE. A mapping of all possible logic* inputs and resulting outputs. A truthtable for a three input AND gate, and a two input OR gate are shown as examples.

3 input AND gate

inputs			output
A	B	C	F
0	0	0	0
0	0	1	0
0	1	0	0
0	1	1	0
1	0	0	0
1	0	1	0
1	1	0	0
1	1	1	1

2 input OR gate (inclusive)

inputs		output
A	B	F
0	0	0
0	1	1
1	0	1
1	1	1

Notice that an output 1 state is obtained from the OR gate when the AND condition is satisfied. For this reason this form of OR gate is known as an *Inclusive* OR gate. An exclusive OR gate does not include the AND condition.

T.T.L. A range of integrated circuits covering about 300 separate packages to perform all manner of logic functions. T.T.L. refers to the manner in which the circuits are constructed using multiples of transistors – Transistor Transistor Logic. Before T.T.L. was developed gates were designed using Resistors and a Transistor. This form of logic circuitry was known as R.T.L. Other forms of logic circuit have been used with varying degrees of popularity but T.T.L. was a head and shoulders winner. Most large manufacturers produced their own T.T.L. family of devices which were standardised into the 7400 series. This refers to the numbering of the devices in the series:–

> 7400 is an I.C. containing 4 two-input NAND gates, 7486 contains 4 two-input EXCLUSIVE OR gates, and so on.

Electronics it would seem cannot be kept simple however. As improvements were demanded by users, and manufacturers developed their processes, various versions of T.T.L. became available with lower power T.T.L., High Speed T.T.L., Schottky T.T.L., in addition to the Standard T.T.L.

V.D.U. The best way to describe this piece of equipment is to compare it with a television set. The numbers, words and characters of programs and messages from the computer are displayed on the screen. The V.D.U. has the disadvantage of not providing a permanent copy, and the number of lines of information displayed is limited. On the other hand they are quiet and cheaper than a full teletype machine.

Typical characteristics:	cost	: keyboard and display £600 – £1,000
	speed	: 60 characters/sec (Faster than T.T.Y. printer)
	print positions	: 80 or 40
	number of lines	: 12, 20, or 24

Notice that these characteristics are only typical, slower, faster, smaller, larger, cheaper, and more costly versions are available.

WORD PROCESSOR. A computer controlled printer. A large memory is capable of storing pages of text which can be reproduced with a single keyboard command. The text can be formatted with paragraphs, spaces, and margins. A popular large business office application is to reproduce standard letters and circulars with a different person's name placed in the appropriate places in each letter printed. The original letter, or pages of text, is entered intially in a conventional manner by a typist at the keyboard.

APPENDIX A

A selection of instructions taken from the instruction set of the Intel 8080 microprocessor.

The descriptive name of the instruction is given on the right hand side of the page, and the assembly language mnemonic is given on the left. The binary form of each instruction and the flags affected are also shown.

The two and three bit fields shown as RP, SSS, and DDD refer to the codings given on page 38 for register pairs, and individual general purpose registers. SSS indicates a *source* register and DDD indicates a *destination* register.

The condition flags are as follows:

Z; Zero Flag
This flag is set to 1 to indicate that execution of an instruction has resulted in all zeroes in the accumulator. The Z flag may also be reset to 0 by the instruction if the result is not zero.

S; Sign Flag
This flag is set equal to bit 7 of the accumulator. Bit 7 is the M.S.B. and will represent the sign of an 8-bit value expressed in 2's complement. A 1 will indicate a negative value and 0 will indicate a positive value.

P; Parity
Parity is determined by counting the number of 1 bits in the accumulator which result from the execution of an instruction. Instructions which affect the parity flag set the flag to 1 for an even number of 1's (even parity) or reset the flag to 0 for an odd number of 1's (odd parity).

CY; Carry Flag
The most basic use of the carry flag is to indicate when an addition instruction causes a 'carry' into the next

higher order digit. The carry flag however can also be used to indicate a 'borrow' condition for a subtraction, or indicate certain logic conditions. (AND OR). Certain other instructions such as RAL and RAR employ the carry flag as a ninth bit in conjunction with the 8-bit accumulator.

AC; Auxiliary Carry
The AC flag is set to 1 if an addition instruction causes a carry from bit 3 of the accumulator. Bit 3 will represent the M.S.B. of a B.C.D. value and thus allows B.C.D. operations to be performed by use of the Decimal Adjust instruction DAA.

The AC flag cannot be tested directly in a program but DAA instruction effectively tests this flag. The DAA instruction thus allows the accumulator to be treated as two 4-bit B.C.D. values. The following example shows how the DAA instruction adds the AC Flag bit (if set) to correct the normal binary addition to B.C.D. format.

38_{10}	= 0011 1000	in 8421 B.C.D.
2_{10}	= 0000 0010	in 8421 B.C.D.
$38_{10} + 2_{10}$	0011 1000	
	0000 0010	
	0011 1010 = $3A_H$	using normal ADD instructions

Clearly $38_{10} + 2_{10} = 40_{10}$ and should give 0100 0000 in B.C.D.

The DAA instruction makes the necessary correction by adding six in B.C.D. to the low-order four bits, and or the four high-order bits, depending upon the B.C.D. values present in the two four bit fields and depending upon the setting of AC flag. The DAA instruction automatically checks out these conditions and adds six if necessary. The result of using the DAA instruction on the above result would be as follows.

0011 1010 +	low order fourbits
0000 0110	greater than 9. add
0100 0000	six
	answer 40_{10} in B.C.D.

Suppose the original addition had been $27_{10} + 9_{10}$

27_{10} = 0010 0111 in B.C.D.

9_{10} = 0000 1001 in B.C.D.

$27_{10} + 9_{10}$ =	0010 0111	
	0000 1001	
	0011 0000 =	30_H or 30 B.C.D. using normal ADD instructions.

This addition however will set the AC flag with the carry from bit 3 to bit 4. Now using the DAA instruction the AC flag will be tested and add one to the high-order four bits.

0011 0000 +	
0000 0110	add 6
0001 0000	auxiliary carry
0100 0110	answer 36_{10} in B.C.D.

These examples are used here to show the use of the AC flag. A more detailed explanation of DAA is given in the instruction set selection which follows.

ACI ADD IMMEDIATE WITH CARRY

Adds the contents of the second byte and the carry bit to the contents of the accumulator

Opcode	Operand
ACI	data

1 1 0 0 1 1 1 0
data (binary)

Flags: Z, S, P, CY, AC

ADC ADD WITH CARRY

Adds one byte of data plus the setting of carryflag (CY) to the contents of the accumulator. The result is stored in the accumulator. ADC then updates the setting of the carry flag to indicate the outcome of the operation.

Add Register to Accumulator with Carry

Opcode	Operand
ADC	register.

The operand must specify one of the registers A through E, H or L. This instruction adds the contents of the specified register and the carry bit to the accumulator and stores the result in the accumulator.

1 0 0 0 1 S S S

Flags: Z, S, P, CY, AC

Add Memory to Accumulator with Carry

Opcode	Operand
ADC	M

Adds the contents of the memory location, whose address is contained in the register pair H – L, and the carry bit to the accumulator and stores the result in the accumulator.

| 1 0 0 0 1 1 1 0 |

Flags: Z, S, P, CY, AC

ADD ADD

Adds one byte of data to the contents of the accumulator. The result is stored in the accumulator. Notice that this instruction excludes the carry flag from the addition but sets the flag to indicate the outcome of the addition.

Add Register to Register

Opcode	Operand
ADD	Register.

The operand must specify one of the registers A through E, H or L. The instruction adds the contents of the specified register to the contents of the accumulator.

| 1 0 0 0 0 S S S |

Flags: Z, S. P, CY, AC

Add from Memory

Opcode	Operand
ADD	M

Adds the contents of the memory location addressed by the H – L register pair to the contents of the accumulator and stores the result in the accumulator. M is a symbolic reference to the H – L register pair.

| 1 0 0 0 0 1 1 0 |

Flags: Z, S, P, CY, AC

ADI — **ADD IMMEDIATE**

Adds the contents of the second byte to the contents of the accumulator and stores the result in the accumulator

Opcode	Operand	
ADI	data	
1 1 0 0 0 1 1 0		1st byte
data (binary)		2nd byte

Flags: Z, S, P. CY, AC

CMC — **COMPLEMENT CARRY**

If the carry flag is set to 0 this instruction will set it to 1. If the carry flag is 1 the instruction resets it to 0. All other flags remain unchanged.

Opcode	Operand
CMC	–
0 0 1 1 1 1 1 1	

Flags: CY only

CMP — **COMPARE WITH ACCUMULATOR**

Compares the specified byte with the contents of the accumulator and indicates the result by setting the carry and zero flags.

The zero flag indicates equality. No carry indicates that the accumulator contains a binary value which is greater than or equal to the specified byte. If the accumulator contents is less than the specified byte the carry flag is set to 1. The meaning of the carry flag is reversed when the values have different signs or one of the values is complemented.

A program can test the condition flags by use of one of the *conditional jump* instructions, such as JZ (Jump if Zero).

Comparisons are performed by subtracting the specified byte from the contents of the accumulator, which is why the zero and carry flags indicate the result. This subtraction uses the internal registers so that both data bytes are preserved. Subtraction employs two's complement addition and so the CMP instruction must re complement the carry flag generated by the subtraction.

Compare Register with Accumulator

Opcode	Operand
CMP	Register

The instruction must specify one of the registers A through E, H or L.

| 1 0 1 1 1 S S S |

Flags: Z, S, P, CY, AC

Compare Memory with Accumulator

Opcode	Operand
CMP	M

The contents of the memory location addressed by the contents of the register pair H – L is compared with the contents of the accumulator. M is a symbolic reference to the memory location pointed to by the register pair H – L.

| 1 0 1 1 1 1 1 0 |

Flags: Z, S, P, CY, AC

Example:

Assume the H – L register pair contains $H = 0\,B_H$
$L = 7\,1_H$

the accumulator contains $2\,A_H$

the memory location $O\,B\,7\,1_H$ contains $E\,B_H$

The instruction C M P M performs the following subtraction

$$\begin{array}{rl} 2A_H = & 0\,0\,1\,0\,1\,0\,1\,0 \\ EB_H = & \underline{1\,1\,1\,0\,1\,0\,1\,1} \end{array} -$$

In fact this subtraction is performed by using 2's C and the true calculation is as follows,

$$\begin{array}{lcll} & \text{CY} & & \\ \text{Accumulator} & \boxed{0} & 0\,0\,1\,0\,1\,0\,1\,0 & + \\ & & \underline{0\,0\,0\,1\,0\,1\,0\,1} & \text{2's C of M} \\ & \boxed{0} & 0\,0\,1\,1\,1\,1\,1\,1 & \end{array}$$

Carry flag $\boxed{1}$
Complemented to give 1, thus indicating that the accumulator is less than the specified memory location.
The two values are <u>not</u> equal and so the zero flag will be 0.

DAA DECIMAL ADJUST ACCUMULATOR

Adjusts the 8-bit accumulator contents to form two four-bit binary coded decimal digits.

Opcode
DAA

| 0 0 1 0 0 1 1 1 |

Flags: Z, S, P. CY, AC

If the least significant four bits of the accumulator have a value greater than nine, or if the AC flag is 1, DAA adds six to the accumulator.

If the most significant four bits of the accumulator have a value greater than nine, or if the carry flag (CY) is 1, DAA adds six to the most significant four bits of the accumulator.

The effect is to convert the hexadecimal results of B.C.D. operations into B.C.D. format.

DCR — **DECREMENT**

Subtracts one from the specified byte. DCR affects all the condition flags except the CY flag.

Opcode	Operand
DCR	Register

| 0 0 D D D 1 0 1 |

Flags: Z, S, P, AC

DCX — **DECREMENT REGISTER PAIR**

Decrements the contents of the specified register pair by one. DCX does not affect any of the condition flags.

Opcode

DCX { B, D, H, SP }

B = B - C register pair
D = D - E register pair
H = H - L register pair
SP = Stack pointer

| 0 0 R P 1 0 1 1 |

Flags: none.

HLT — HALT

Halts the microprocessor's program operation.
The program counter contains the address of the next sequential instruction. The flags and registers remain unchanged.

| 0 1 1 1 0 1 1 0 |

Flags: none.

INX — INCREMENT REGISTER PAIR

INX adds one to the contents of the specified register pair. INX affects none of the condition flags.

Opcode	Operand
INX	B, D, H, SP

| 0 0 R P 0 0 1 1 |

Flags: none

JC — JUMP IF CARRY

Tests the state of the carryflag. If the flag is set to 1, the program resumes at the address specified in the two byte address of the three byte instruction. If the flag is reset to 0 program execution continues with the next sequential instruction.

Opcode	Operand
JC	address

1 1 0 1 1 0 1 0	1st byte
low-order address	2nd byte
high-order address	3rd byte

JC (Continued)

Flags: none

JM **JUMP IF MINUS**

Tests the setting of the sign flag. If the contents of the accumulator are negative (sign flag = 1) program execution resumes at the address specified in the JM instruction. If the contents of the accumulator are positive (sign flag = 0) execution continues with the next sequential instruction.

Opcode JM	Operand address
1 1 1 1 1 0 1 0	1st byte
low-order address	2nd byte
high-order address	3rd byte

Flags: none

JMP **JUMP**

Performs a program *jump* by loading the address given by the second and third bytes into the program counter.

Opcode JMP	Operand address
1 1 0 0 0 0 1 1	1st byte
low-order address	2nd byte
high-order address	3rd byte

Flags: none

JNC **JUMP IF NO CARRY**

Tests the setting of the carry flag. If there is no carry (carry flag = 0), program execution resumes at the address specified in the second and third bytes of the three byte instruction. If the carry flag is set to 1 execution of the program continues with the next sequential instruction.

1 1 0 1 0 0 1 0	1st byte
low-order address	2nd byte
high-order address	3rd byte

Flags: none

JZ **JUMP IF ZERO**

Tests the setting of the zero flag. If the flag is set to 1 program execution resumes at the address specified in the JZ instruction. If the flat is reset to 0 execution continues with the next sequential instruction.

Opcode	Operand
JZ	address

1 1 0 0 1 0 1 0	1st byte
low-order address	2nd byte
high-order address	3rd byte

Flags: none

LDA **LOAD ACCUMULATOR DIRECT**

A copy of the data held in the memory location whose address is given by bytes two and three is loaded into the accumulator.

Opcode	Operand
LDA	address

0 0 1 1 1 0 1 0	1st byte
low-order address	2nd byte
high-order address	3rd byte

Flags: none

LHLD — LOAD H AND L DIRECT

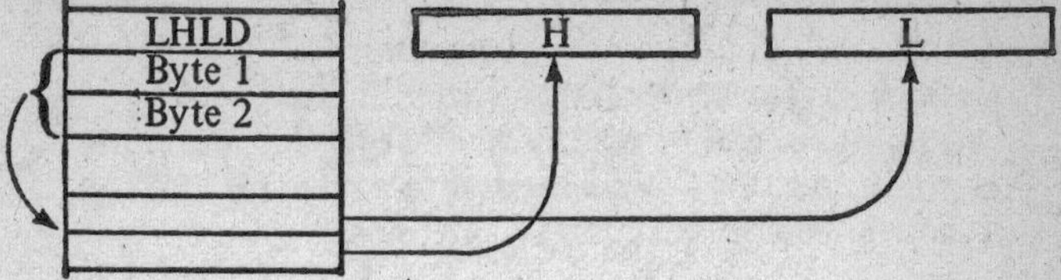

A copy of the byte stored in the location whose address is specified by bytes two and three of the three byte instruction is loaded into the L register. The byte held in the next memory location is loaded into the H register.

Opcode	Operand
LHLD	address

0 0 1 0 1 0 1 0	1st byte
low-order address	2nd byte
high-order address	3rd byte

Flags: none

LXI — LOAD REGISTER PAIR IMMEDIATE

The second and third bytes of the instruction are loaded into a specified register pair. The specified register pair is defined by the code given on page xx and represented by RP in the instruction.

Opcode	Operand	
LXI	{B, D, H, SP}	data

0 0 R P 0 0 0 1	1st byte
low-order data	2nd byte
high-order data	3rd byte

Flags: none

Moves a byte of data by copying a *source* of data into a *destination*. The source data remains unchanged. The instructions operands specify whether the move is from register to register, from a register to a memory location, or from a memory location to a register.

Move Register to Register

Opcode	Operand
MOV	reg 1, reg 2

The contents of reg 2 is copied into register 1.

0 1 D D D S S S

Flags: none

Move to Memory

Opcode	Operand
MOV	M,r

The contents of the specified register is copied into the memory location whose address is held in the register pair H - L. MOV memory to memory is not possible.

0 1 1 1 0 S S S

Flags: none

Move from Memory

Opcode	Operand
MOV	r, M

The contents of the memory location whose address is held in register pair H - L is copied into the specified register. M is a symbolic reference to memory.

0 1 D D D 1 1 0

Flags: none

MVI **MOVE IMMEDIATE**

Move Immediate to Register

Opcode	Operand
MVI	reg. data

The data byte held in the second byte of the instruction is copied into the specified register.

0 0 D D D 1 1 0	1st byte
data.	2nd byte

Flags: none

Move Immediate to Memory

Opcode	Operand
MVI	M, data

The data stored in the second byte of the instruction is copied into the memory location whose address is held in register pair H - L.

0 0 1 1 0 1 1 0	1st byte
data.	2nd byte

Flags: none

PCHL **MOVE H and L TO PROGRAM COUNTER**

This instruction has the effect of a jump instruction.

Opcode
PCHL

|1 1 1 0 1 0 0 1|

Flags: none

RAL ROTATE LEFT THROUGH CARRY

Rotates the contents of the accumulator and the carry flag one bit position to the left. The carry flag is treated as part of the accumulator and its content is moved into the L.S.B. of the accumulator which is vacated as the accumulator bits move left. The M.S.B. of accumulator is transferred to the carry flag. The diagram illustrates the operation.

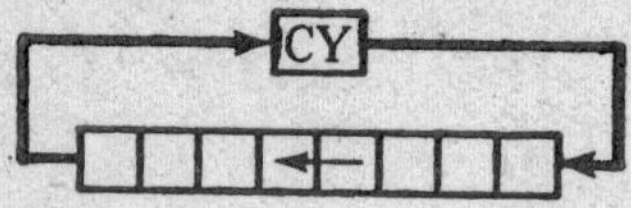

Opcode	Operand
RAL	–

|0 0 0 1 0 1 1 1|

Flags: CY only.

RAR ROTATE RIGHT THROUGH CARRY

Rotates the contents of the accumulator and carry flag one bit position to the right The diagram illustrates the operation.

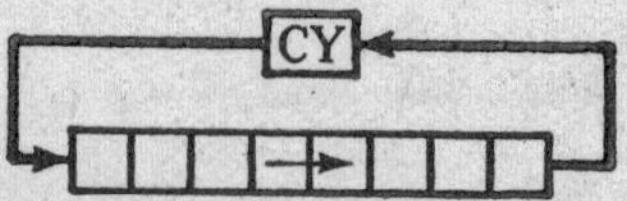

Opcode
RAR

|0 0 0 1 1 1 1 1|

Flags: CY only.

RLC ROTATE ACCUMULATOR LEFT

The carry flag is set equal to the high-order bit of the accumulator, overwriting its previous setting. The contents of the accumulator is then shifted one bit position to the left with the high-order bit transferring to the low-order bit position of the accumulator.

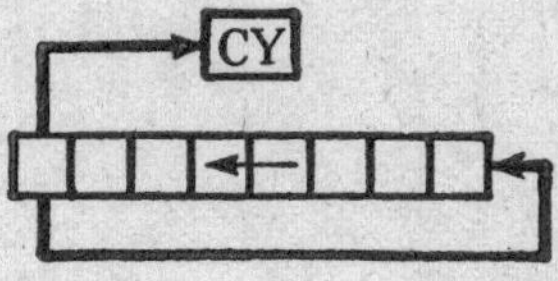

Opcode	Operand
RLC	–

|0 0 0 0 0 1 1 1|

Flags: CY only.

RRC ROTATE ACCUMULATOR RIGHT

The carry flag is set equal to the low-order bit of the accumulator, overwriting its previous setting. The contents of the accumulator is then shifted one bit position to the right with the low order bit transferring to the high-order bit position of the accumulator. The diagram illustrates the operation.

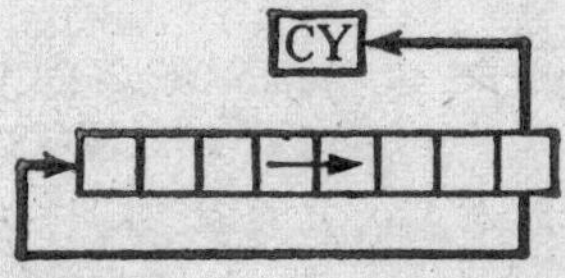

Opcode	Operand
RRC	–

|0 0 0 0 1 1 1 1|

Flags: CY only.

SBI — SUBTRACT IMMEDIATE WITH BORROW

The contents of the second byte of the instruction and the carry flag is subtracted from the contents of the accumulator. The result is stored in the accumulator.

Opcode	Operand
SBI	data

| 1 1 0 1 1 1 1 0 |

Flags: Z, S, P, CY, AC

STA — STORE ACCUMULATOR DIRECT

A copy of the contents of the accumulator is loaded into the memory location specified in the second and third bytes of the three byte instruction.

Opcode	Operand
STA	address

| 0 0 1 1 0 0 1 0 |
| low-order address |
| high-order address |

Flags: none

STAX — STORE ACCUMULATOR INDIRECT

A copy of the contents of the accumulator is loaded into the memory location addressed by register pair B-C or D-E.

Opcode	Operand
STAX	{B, D}

| 0 0 0 r 0 0 1 0 |

Flags: none r = 0 for register pair B-C
r = 1 for register pair D-E

STC **SET CARRY**

Sets the carry flag to 1.

Opcode	Operand
STC	–

| 0 0 1 1 0 1 1 1 |

Flag: CY only.

SUB **SUBTRACT**

Subtracts one data byte from the contents of the accumulator. The result is stored in the accumulator. The SUB instruction employs 2's C arithmetic to perform the subtraction.

Subtract Register from Accumulator

Opcode	Operand
SUB	Register

The instruction must specify a register A through E, H or L. The contents of the specified register is subtracted from the accumulator.

| 1 0 0 1 0 S S S |

Flags: Z, S, P, CY, AC

Subtract Memory from Accumulator

Opcode	Operand
SUB	M

The contents of the memory location whose address is held in register pair H - L is subtracted from the contents of the accumulator. The result is stored in the accumulator. M is a symbolic reference to a memory location.

| 1 0 0 1 0 1 1 0 |

Flags: Z, S, P. CY, AC

SUI SUBTRACT IMMEDIATE

The contents of the second byte of the instruction is subtracted from the contents of the accumulator.

Opcode	Operand
SUI	data

1 1 0 1 0 1 1 0	1st byte
data	2nd byte

Flags: Z, S. P. CY, AC

XCHG EXCHANGE H and L WITH D and E

Exchanges the contents of H and D registers, and exchanges the contents of L and E registers.

Opcode	Operand
XCHG	–

| 1 1 1 0 1 0 1 1 |

Flags: none.

EXERCISES

The following questions will help to reinforce the main ideas discussed in the text. A sample solution, and answers to all questions are given at the back of the book. Readers are urged not to make reference to these until a good attempt had been made to produce his, or her, own answer. To avoid inadvertently seeing the answers before attempting a question the answers have been given on separate pages.

A study of the selection of instructions taken from the instruction set of the Intel 8080 microprocessor, and given in Appendix A, will serve as an extension to the main text. Notice the setting of *flags** performed by some instructions and the testing of these *flags* by others. Also notice how some instructions make reference to a memory location for the operand by using the register pair H - L as a *pointer.*

QUESTIONS

Q.1. Convert the following decimal values to binary form as stored in an 8-bit register.

i) 22
ii) 86
iii) 120
iv) 39
v) 95
vi) 255

Q.2. Convert each of the binary values found in Q1 to :–

a) Octal code
b) Hexadecimal code
c) 1's complement.

Q.3. Convert the decimal values of Q1 to 8421 B.C.D.

Q.4. Convert the following HEX values to 8-bit binary form

i) 7A
ii) BB
iii) 3D
iv) C2
v) 4F
vi) EA

Q.5. Convert each of the binary values found in Q4 to 2's complement and hence subtract each of the original hexidecimal values from FD_H.

Q.6. State the Boolean logic expression for each of the gate circuits shown and construct a truth table for each circuit.

(i)

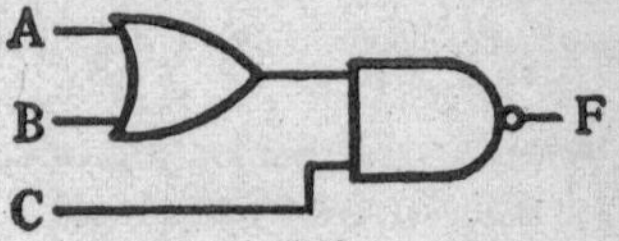

(ii)

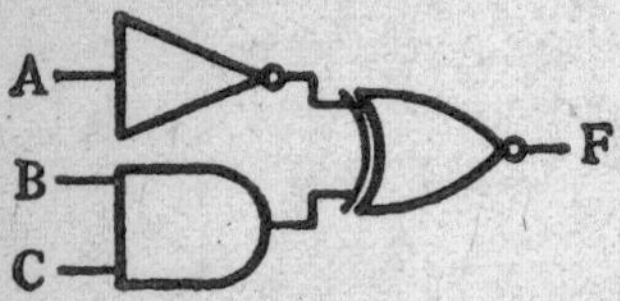

(iii)

(iv)

Q.7. Name the four main sections of a computer.

Q.8. Why is the address bus of an 8-bit microprocessor 16-bits wide?

Q.9. Explain briefly the function of each of the microprocessor sections listed.

Memory
Decode circuit
A.L.U.
Accumulator
General Purpose Registers
Flags
Program Counter
Stack Pointer

Q.10. Give simple meanings for the following terms:

i) Instruction
ii) Operand
iii) Machine Language
iv) Memory Map
v) Interface
vi) Handshake

Q.10 (Continued)

vii) Byte
viii) R.A.M.
xi) Interrupt
x) Latch
xi) Two-byte instruction
xii) Three-byte instruction
xiii) High Level Language
xiv) Instruction set
xv) Peripherals
xvi) Bit
xvii) R.O.M.
xviii) P.R.O.M.
xix) Enable
xx) C.P.U.

Q.11. Using the selection from the Intel 8080 instruction set given in Appendix A construct a program to perform the following tasks in the sequence shown.

i) Load memory locations 0 0 A A_H, 0 0 A B_H and 0 0 A C_H with the values 76_{10}, 35_{10} and 21_{10} respectively.

ii) Add 15_{10} to the contents of location 0 0 A A_H.

iii) Subtract 20_{10} from location 0 0 A B_H.

iv) Add the contents of locations 0 0 A A_H, 0 0 A B_H, 0 0 A C_H, and store the result in location A D_H.

v) END

The starting address of the program is to be 0 0 0 0.

Q.12. Construct a program to take the contents of ten sequential memory locations, divide by two each value which is equal to, or greater than, 20_{10}, or multiply by two each value which is less than 20_{10}, and store each new modified value in a new sequential set of memory locations. The original ten data values can be assumed to be stored in a memory block starting at location $1\,0\,0\,0_{10}$ and the starting address for the modified values is to be $2\,0\,0\,0_{10}$.

Q. 12 (Continued)

This program is not quite so straightforward as the one given in question 11. A few hints will be helpful, and give an opportunity to show the use of a *flow chart*. The program involves the use of a *loop* and a *counter*. Remember shifting a binary number left and right by one bit multiplies and divides by two respectively.

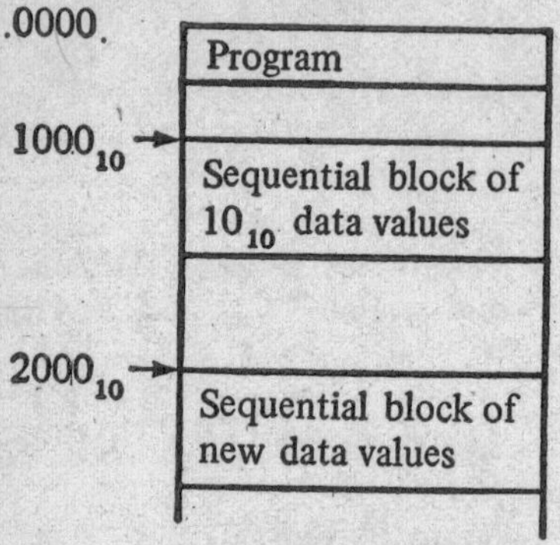

Program memory map.

Q. 12 (Continued)

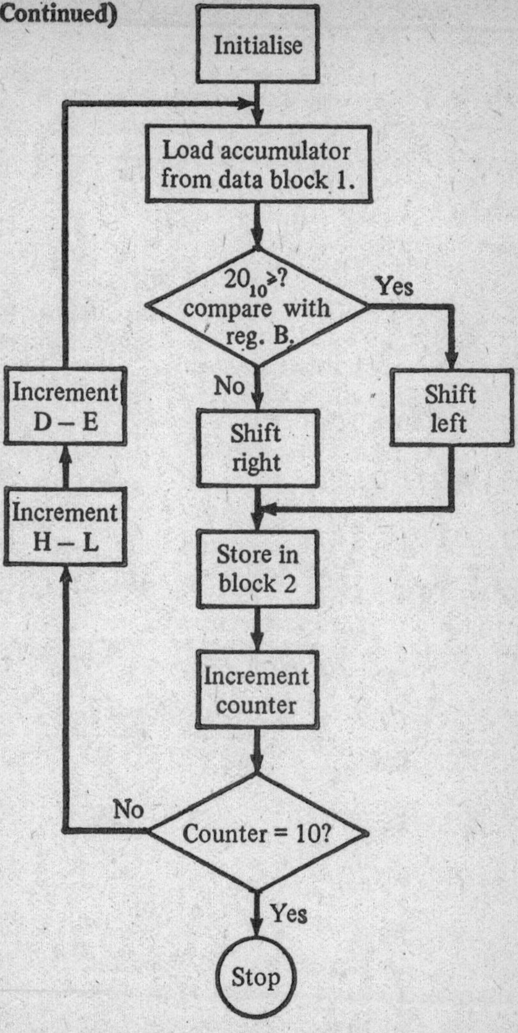

Suggested flow chart for program. INITIALISATION will include: loading 20_{10} into a register (register B.), setting memory pointers (H – L and D – E register pairs), and setting counter to zero (register C).

SOLUTIONS AND ANSWERS TO QUESTIONS 1 – 12.

Q.1. i)

2	)2 2	remainder
÷2	1 1	0
÷2	5	1
÷2	2	1
÷2	1	0
	0	1

$= 10110_2$

or 00010110 in an 8-bit register

ii) 00110110

iii) 01111000

iv) 00100111

v) 01011111

vi) 11111111

Q.2. a) i) $\underbrace{00}_{0}\ \underbrace{010}_{2}\ \underbrace{110}_{6}$ in octal

ii) 066_8

iii) 170_8

iv) 047_8

v) 137_8

vi) 377_8

b) i) $\underbrace{0001}_{1}\ \underbrace{0110}_{6}$ in hexadecimal

ii) 36_H

iii) 78_H

iv) 27_H

v) $5F_H$

vi) FF_H

c) i) 11111111
00010110

11101001 = 1's C of 00010110

ii) 11001001

iii) 10000111

iv) 11011000

v) 10100000

vi) 00000000

Q.3. i) 0 2 2_{10}

0000 0010 0010 in 8421 B.C.D.

ii) 000010000110

iii) 000100100000

iv) 000000111001

v) 000010010101

vi) 001001010101

Q.4. i) $7\,A_{HEX}$

0111   1010   Each HEX digit represent four binary digits.

ii) 10111011   in binary

iii) 00111101

iv) 11000010

v) 01001111

vi) 11101010

Q.5. i) 01111010_2 to 2's C. Convert to 1's C and add 1.

```
 11111111
 01111010
 --------
 10000101
        1  +
 --------
 10000110   = 2's C of 7 A(HEX)
```

Now to subtract $7\,A_{HEX}$ from $F\,D_{HEX}$ the 2's C of $7\,A_{HEX}$ is added to the binary value of $F\,D_{HEX}$

```
F D(HEX) =     11111101
               10000110  +
               --------
carry    [1]   10000011 = 1 + 2 + 128 =
                                   131(10)
```

Check $F\,D_{HEX} = 53_{10}$

$7\,A_{HEX} = 122_{10}$

ii) 01000010 = $2 + 64 = 66_{10}$

iii) 11000000 = 192_{10}

iv) 00111011 = 59_{10}

v) 10101110 = 174_{10}

vi) 00010011 = 19_{10}

Q.6. i) $F = (A.B.C) + D$

A B C D	F
0 0 0 0	0
0 0 0 1	1
0 0 1 0	0
0 0 1 1	1
0 1 0 0	0
0 1 0 1	1
0 1 1 0	0
0 1 1 1	1
1 0 0 0	0
1 0 0 1	1
1 0 1 0	0
1 0 1 1	1
1 1 0 0	0
1 1 0 1	1
1 1 1 0	1
1 1 1 1	1

to cover every possible combination of 0's and 1's for inputs A B C and D notice the pattern of the 0's and 1's in the column of the table; alternate in D column, two's in C, fours in B, and eights in A.

ii) $F = \overline{(A + B).C}$

A B C	$\overline{F}$ F
0 0 0	0 1
0 0 1	0 1
0 1 0	0 1
0 1 1	1 0
1 0 0	0 1
1 0 1	1 0
1 1 0	0 1
1 1 1	1 0

Notice that if $F = \overline{(A+B).C}$ then $\overline{F} = (A+B).C$
It may therefore be found easy to determine $\overline{F}$ for each case and then take the complement to obtain F.

iii) $F = \bar{A} \oplus B.C.$ Notice the use of the Exclusive OR symbol. $\oplus$

A B C	F
0 0 0	1
0 0 1	1
0 1 0	1
0 1 1	0
1 0 0	0
1 0 1	0
1 1 0	0
1 1 1	1

iv) $F = \overline{A.B} + C$

A B C	F
0 0 0	1
0 0 1	1
0 1 0	0
0 1 1	1
1 0 0	0
1 0 1	1
1 1 0	1
1 1 1	0

Q.7. 1 C.P.U.
2 Memory
3 Input/Output (1/0)
4 Control.

Q.8. An 8-bit address will only cover the range of values from 0 to 255_{10}

$$11111111_2 = 2^0 + 2^1 + 2^2 + 2^3 + 2^4 + 2^5 + 2^6 + 2^7$$
$$= 1 + 2 + 4 + 8 + 16 + 32 + 64 + 128$$
$$= 255_{10}$$

Including zero therefore the maximum number of locations which can be addressed will be 256_{10}. Using 16-bits the total number will be 65536_{10} which permits 65k memory locations to be addressed.

Q.9. Refer to main text if you are unable to answer with confidence.

Q.10. Refer to main text if you are unable to answer with confidence.

Q.11. Program

Memory Location (Hexadecimal)	Instruction Mnemonic		Instruction Machine Language
0 0 0 0	LXI	H	0 0 R P 0 0 0 1
0 0 0 1		A A	1 0 1 0 1 0 1 0
0 0 0 2		0 0	0 0 0 0 0 0 0 0
0 0 0 3	MVI	M	0 0 1 1 0 1 1 0
0 0 0 4		4 C	0 1 0 0 1 1 0 0
0 0 0 5	INX	H	0 0 R P 0 0 1 1
0 0 0 6	MVI	M	0 0 1 1 0 1 1 0
0 0 0 7		2 3	0 0 1 0 0 0 1 1
0 0 0 8	INX	H	0 0 R P 0 0 1 1
0 0 0 9	MVI	M	0 0 1 1 0 1 1 0
0 0 0 A		1 5	0 0 0 1 0 1 0 1

Comments

H – L register pair set to point to location 0 0 A A.
Loads 76_{10}, 35_{10}, 21_{10} into locations 0 0 A A, 0 0 A B 0 0 A C respectively.
R P is the coding for register pair H – L.
H – L is incremented to point 0 0 A B and 0 0 A C.

0 0 0 B	LXI	H	0 0 R P 0 0 0 1
0 0 0 C		A A	1 0 1 0 1 0 1 0
0 0 0 D		0 0	0 0 0 0 0 0 0 0
0 0 0 E	MOV	r, M	0 1 D D D 1 1 0
0 0 0 F	ACI		1 1 0 0 1 1 1 0
0 0 1 0		O F	0 0 0 0 1 1 1 1
0 0 1 1	MOV	M, r	0 1 1 1 0 S S S

Comments

RP is coding for H – L.
D D D is coding for Accumulator.

Add 15_{10} to location 0 0 A A by first moving contents of 0 0 A A to the accumulator and adding 15_{10}. The result is then replaced in 0 0 A A.

0 0 1 2	LXI	H	0 0 R P 0 0 0 1
0 0 1 3		A B	1 0 1 0 1 0 1 1
0 0 1 4		0 0	0 0 0 0 0 0 0 0
0 0 1 5	MOV	r, M	0 1 D D D 1 1 0
0 0 1 6	SBI		1 1 0 1 1 1 1 0
0 0 1 7		1 4	0 0 0 1 0 1 0 0
0 0 1 8	MOV	M, r	0 1 1 1 0 S S S

Comments

H – L set to point to location 0 0 A B. Contents of 0 0 A B moved to accumulator and 20_{10} subtracted. Result is returned to location 0 0 A B.
D D D and S S S are codings for accumulator.

0 0 1 9	LXI	H	0 0 R P 0 0 0 1
0 0 1 A		A A	1 0 1 0 1 0 1 0
0 0 1 B		0 0	0 0 0 0 0 0 0 0
0 0 1 C	MOV	r, M	0 1 D D D 1 1 0
0 0 1 D	INX	H	0 0 R P 0 0 1 1
0 0 1 E	ADC	M	1 0 0 0 1 1 1 0
0 0 1 F	INX	H	0 0 R P 0 0 1 1
0 0 2 0	ADC	M	1 0 0 0 1 1 1 0
0 0 2 1	LXI	H	0 0 R P 0 0 0 1
0 0 2 2		A D	1 0 1 0 1 1 0 1
0 0 2 3		0 0	0 0 0 0 0 0 0 0
0 0 2 4	MOV	M, r	0 1 1 1 0 S S S

Comments

H – L register pair used to point to location 0 0 A A. Contents of 0 0 A A entered into accumulator. H – L incremented to point to 0 0 A B and contents added to accumulator.
H – L incremented to point to 0 0 A C and contents of 0 0 A C added to accumulator.
The sum is returned to memory location 0 0 A D.

0 0 2 5	HLT	0 1 1 1 0 1 1 0

Comments

Halt

Q.12. Program. A suggested approach, there are variations possible.

Memory Location (HEX)	Instruction Mnemonic		Machine Language
0000	MVI	B	0 0 D D D 1 1 0
0001		14	0 0 0 1 0 1 0 0

Comments

Register B loaded with 20_{10}

D D D = code for register B.

0002	MVI	C	0 0 D D D 1 1 0
0003		00	0 0 0 0 0 0 0 0

Comments

Set counter (register C) to zero.

D D D code for register C.

0004	LXI	H	0 0 RP 0 0 0 1

Comments

R P is code for H – L

0005		E8	1 1 1 0 1 0 0 0
0006		03	0 0 0 0 0 0 1 1
0007	LXI	D	0 0 R P 0 0 0 1

Comments

R P is code for D – E

0008		D0	1 1 0 1 0 0 0 0
0009		07	0 0 0 0 0 1 1 1
000A	MOV	r, M	0 1 D D D 1 1 0

Comments

D D D is code for accumulator

0 0 0 B	CMP B	1 0 1 1 1 S S S

Comments
S S S is code for register B.

0 0 0 C	JNC	1 1 0 1 0 0 1 0
0 0 0 D	1 4	0 0 0 1 0 1 0 0
0 0 0 E	0 0	0 0 0 0 0 0 0 0

Comments
If carry flag not set by CMP B instruction then program jumps to location 0 0 1 4_H.

0 0 0 F	CMC	0 0 1 1 1 1 1 1

Comments
Sets carry bit to 0

0 0 1 0	RAL	0 0 0 1 0 1 1 1

Comments
x 2

0 0 1 1	JMP	1 1 0 0 0 0 1 1

Comments
JMP to location 0 0 1 5_H

0 0 1 2	1 5	1 0 1 0 0 1 0 1
0 0 1 3	0 0	0 0 0 0 0 0 0 0
0 0 1 4	RAR	0 0 0 1 1 1 1 1

Comments
÷ 2

0 0 1 5	XCHG	1 1 1 0 1 0 1 1
0 0 1 6	MOV M, r	0 1 1 1 0 S S S
0 0 1 7	XCHG	1 1 1 0 1 0 1 1

Comments
Move contents of D – E to H – L to act as block 2 pointer . . . and back again

0 0 1 8	INR C	0 0 D D D 1 0 0

Comments
Increment counter reg. C

0 0 1 9	MVI	A	0 0 D D D 1 1 0
0 0 1 A		0 A	0 0 0 0 1 0 1 0
0 0 1 B		0 0	0 0 0 0 0 0 0 0

Comments
The value 10_{10} is entered into the accumulator. D D D is the code for the accumulator.

0 0 1 C	CMP	C	1 0 1 1 1 S S S
0 0 1 D	JZ		1 1 0 0 1 0 1 0
0 0 1 E		B 5	1 0 1 1 0 1 0 1
0 0 1 F		0 0	0 0 0 0 0 0 0 0

Comments
Compare acc. with reg. C (counter). If register C contains 10_{10} then CMP instruction will set zero flag. JZ tests this flag and if set jumps to HALT.

0 0 2 0	INX	H	0 0 R P 0 0 1 1

Comments
Increments H – L register pair

0 0 2 1	INX	D	0 0 R P 0 0 1 1

Comments
Increments D – E register pair

0 0 2 2	JMP		1 1 0 0 0 0 1 1
0 0 2 3		0 A	0 0 0 0 1 0 1 0
0 0 2 4		0 0	0 0 0 0 0 0 0 0

Comments
Jump to location 0 0 0 A. This loop repeated until counter reaches 10_{10}.

0 0 2 5	HLT		0 1 1 1 0 1 1 0

Comments
Halt.

BP1	First Book of Transistor Equivalents and Substitutes	60p
BP2	Handbook of Radio, TV and Ind. & Transmitting Tube & Valve Equiv.	60p
BP6	Engineers and Machinists Reference Tables	50p
BP7	Radio and Electronic Colour Codes and Data Chart	25p
BP11	Practical Transistor Novelty Circuits	40p
BP14	Second Book of Transistor Equivalents	1.10p
BP22	79 Electronic Novelty Circuits	1.00p
BP23	First Book of Practical Electronic Projects	75p
BP24	52 Projects using IC741	95p
BP25	How to Build Your Own Electronic and Quartz Controlled Watches & Clocks	85p
BP26	Radio Antenna Handbook for Long Distance Reception & Transmission	85p
BP27	Giant Chart of Radio Electronic Semiconductor & Logic Symbols	60p
BP28	Resistor Selection Handbook (International Edition)	60p
BP29	Major Solid State Audio Hi-Fi Construction Projects	85p
BP30	Two Transistor Electronic Projects	85p
BP31	Practical Electical Re-wiring & Repairs	85p
BP32	How to Build Your Own Metal and Treasure Locators	1.00p
BP33	Electronic Calculator Users Handbook	95p
BP34	Practical Repair & Renovation of Colour TV's	1.25p
BP35	Handbook of IC Audio Preamplifier & Power Amplifier Construction	1.25p
BP36	50 Circuits Using Germanium, Silicon and Zener Diodes	75p
BP37	50 Projects Using Relays, SCR's and TRIAC's	1.25p
BP38	Fun & Games with your Electronic Calculator	75p
BP39	50 (FET) Field Effect Transistor Projects	1.25p
BP40	Digital IC Equivalents and Pin Connections	2.50p
BP41	Linear IC Equivalents and Pin Connections	2.75p
BP42	50 Simple L.E.D. Circuits	75p
BP43	How to make Walkie-Talkies	1.25p
BP44	IC 555 Projects	1.75p
BP45	Projects on Opto-Electronics	1.25p
BP46	Radio Circuits using IC's	1.35p
BP47	Mobile Discotheque Handbook	1.35p
BP48	Electronic Projects for Beginners	1.35p
BP49	Popular Electronic Projects	1.45p
BP50	IC LM3900 Projects	1.35p
BP51	Electronic Music and Creative Tape Recording	1.25p
BP52	Long Distance Television Reception (TV–DX) for the Enthusiast	1.45p
BP53	Practical Electronic Calculations and Formulae	2.25p
BP54	Your Electronic Calculator and Your Money	1.35p
BP55	Radio Stations Guide	1.45p
BP56	Electronic Security Devices	1.45p
BP57	How to Build your own Solid State Oscilloscope	1.50p
BP58	50 Circuits using 7400 Series IC's	1.35p
BP59	Second Book of CMOS IC Projects	1.50p
BP60	Practical Construction of Pre-Amps, Tone Controls, Filters and Attenuators	1.45p
BP61	Beginners Guide to Digital Techniques	95p
BP62	Elements of Electronics – Book 1	2.25p
BP63	Elements of Electronics – Book 2	2.25p
BP64	Elements of Electronics – Book 3	2.25p
BP65	Single IC Projects	1.50p
BP66	Beginners Guide to Microprocessors and Computing	N.Y.A.
BP67	Counter Driver and Numeral Display Projects	N.Y.A.
BP68	Choosing and Using Your Hi-Fi	N.Y.A.
BP69	Electronic Games	N.Y.A.
126	Boys Book of Crystal Sets	25p
160	Coil Design and Construction Manual	75p
196	AF–RF Reactance – Frequency Chart for Constructors	15p
200	Handbook of Practical Electronic Musical Novelties	50p
201	Practical Transistorised Novelties for Hi-Fi Enthusiasts	35p
202	Handbook of Integrated Circuits (IC's) Equivalents and Substitutes	1.00p
203	IC's and Transistor Gadgets Construction Handbook	60p
205	First Book of Hi-Fi Loudspeaker Enclosures	75p
207	Practical Electronic Science Projects	75p
208	Practical Stereo and Quadrophony Handbook	75p
210	The Complete Car Radio Manual	1.00p
211	First Book of Diode Characteristics Equivalents and Substitutes	1.25p
213	Electronic Circuits for Model Railways	1.00p
214	Audio Enthusiasts Handbook	85p
215	Shortwave Circuits and Gear for Experimenters and Radio Hams	85p
217	Solid State Power Supply Handbook	85p
218	Build Your Own Electronic Experimenters Laboratory	85p
219	Solid State Novelty Projects	85p
220	Build Your Own Solid State Hi-Fi and Audio Accessories	85p
221	28 Tested Transistor Projects	95p
222	Solid State Short Wave Receivers for Beginners	95p
223	50 Projects using IC CA3130	95p
224	50 CMOS IC Projects	95p
225	A Practical Introduction to Digital IC's	95p
226	How to Build Advanced Short Wave Receivers	1.20p
227	Beginners Guide to Building Electronic Projects	1.25p
228	Essential Theory for the Electronics Hobbyist	1.25p